How to See Like a Machine

How to See Like a Machine

Images After AI

Trevor Paglen

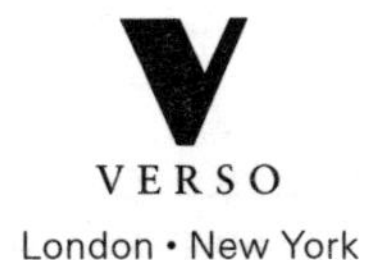

London • New York

First published by Verso 2026

The manufacturer's authorized representative in the EU for product safety (GPSR) is LOGOS EUROPE, 9 rue Nicolas Poussin, 17000, La Rochelle, France
contact@logoseurope.eu

3 5 7 9 10 8 6 4 2

Verso
UK: 6 Meard Street, London W1F 0EG
US: 207 East 32nd Street, New York, NY 10016
versobooks.com

Verso is the imprint of New Left Books

ISBN-13: 978-1-83674-216-6
ISBN-13: 978-1-83674-218-0 (UK EBK)
ISBN-13: 978-1-83674-219-7 (US EBK)

British Library Cataloguing in Publication Data
A catalogue record for this book is available from the British Library

Library of Congress Cataloging-in-Publication Data

Names: Paglen, Trevor author
Title: How to see like a machine : images after AI / Trevor Paglen.
Description: London : Verso, 2026. | Includes bibliographical references and index.
Identifiers: LCCN 2026004217 (print) | LCCN 2026004218 (ebook) | ISBN 9781836742166 hardback | ISBN 9781836742197 ebook
Subjects: LCSH: Image (Philosophy) | Generative artificial intelligence—Social aspects
Classification: LCC B105.I47 P34 2026 (print) | LCC B105.I47 (ebook)
LC record available at https://lccn.loc.gov/2026004217
LC ebook record available at https://lccn.loc.gov/2026004218

Typeset in Sabon by MJ & N Gavan, Truro, Cornwall
Printed and bound by CPI Group (UK) Ltd, Croydon CR0 4YY

Contents

Introduction

At first, I didn't get it. I figured it might turn into a Photoshop plugin one day. One that no self-respecting artist would ever use. But I was wrong. I thought I was seeing a ripple on the ocean's horizon. Turns out, a tidal wave was forming. In the mid-2010s, at my then-studio in an old Berlin *Altbau* overlooking Torstrasse, my assistants and I were learning how to see like a machine. We were building a software framework for doing computer vision. We had gotten our hands on some then-powerful graphics processing units (GPUs), and the system was beginning to fire.

We pointed a webcam out the window. A series of green lines outlined buildings and streets, mapping the urban terrains as if the camera were a guided missile plotting a route to its target. With a few keystrokes the system changed mode and began to draw bounding boxes around cars and pedestrians, reading the license plate of every vehicle that drove by, tracking them like targets in a Predator drone's crosshairs. More keystrokes. A camera in the studio identified each of our faces, guessing what sorts of moods we were in by analyzing our micro-expressions, and began an automated inventory of studio clutter: books, tables, sculptures, computer monitors, keyboards, drawings, and coffee mugs.

Our software collapsed the visual field into a world of vectors and mathematical abstractions. We could even watch the real-time raw data—an impossibly fast, *Matrix*-like cascade of scrolling numbers.

But it could do much more. We could probe the inner workings of algorithms themselves. We could train a facial recognition system on a historical figure like Frantz Fanon or Simone de Beauvoir and watch it generate ghostly images of their faces. The algorithm was showing us the shapes and textures it was looking for when it tried to identify a specific person. We could do the same for objects, revealing what the classifier considered the Platonic forms of apples, stealth bombers, religious altars, sharks, the sun. We could go deeper still, tapping into the hidden layers of neural networks, visualizing the abstract shapes and textures that would maximally activate individual neurons. We could see into a world of invisible images—images that computer algorithms made for themselves in their attempts to translate the world of human visual perception into the quantified world of computers.

Leif Ryge, our lead developer, named the framework "Chair" because using it was like sitting in the captain's chair of the starship *Enterprise*—surveying the universe through an array of sensors, scanning for life-forms, identifying unknown

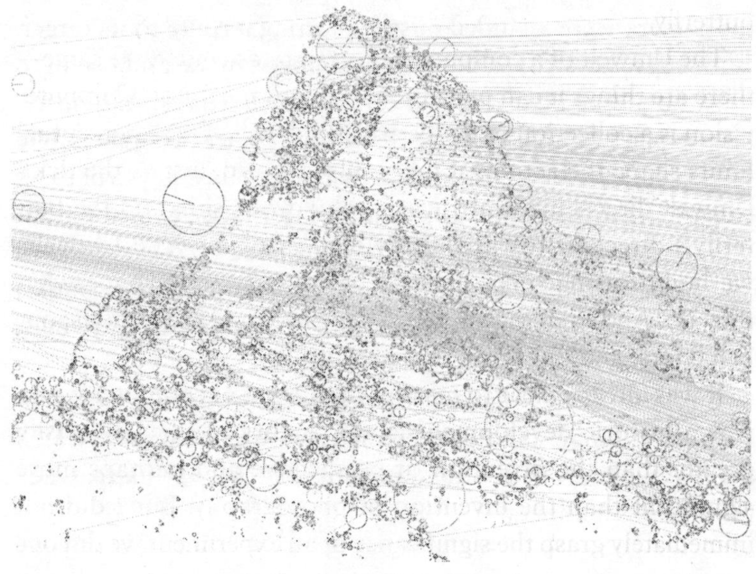

vessels, communicating with aliens, locking photon torpedoes onto enemy spacecraft, or plotting a jump across the galaxy. In the captain's chair, the ship's vast sensorium merges with human perception.

Looking at the world through Chair was like putting on a pair of glasses to experience an alternative version of reality, or temporarily inhabiting the sensorium—the *Umwelt*—of a robot, an animal, or an alien. The concept of Umwelt—coined by the early twentieth-century biosemiotician Jakob von Uexküll—describes how the perceptual apparatus of different animals creates a different reality for each of them.[1] A dog's acute sense of smell creates an entirely different reality for it than that of a dolphin, which has no sense of smell at all; the world of a tick is dominated by the scent of butyric acid emanating from the hair follicles of mammals, and a deep sensitivity to temperatures around 37 degrees Celsius (a signal of nourishment in the form of warm blood). The world of an owl monkey, with its monochromatic vision, is completely devoid of color, while a trichromatic human cannot experience the far larger world of colors in the Umwelt of a pentachromatic butterfly.

The Umwelt of a computer vision system is much the same—there are things it can perceive and things it cannot. Computer vision is a collection of lenses and blindfolds. These perceptual limits shape the actions it takes in the world, just as the tick's Umwelt directs it toward warm, blood-rich skin and the butterfly's directs it toward ultraviolet blossoms. The Umwelts we build for machines define what they see and shape what they do. And in doing so, they shape us—our institutions, our behaviors, and our sense of reality itself.

It was already clear to me that the advent of computer vision was a historic development in the history of images—easily greater than the invention of perspective and perhaps more significant than the invention of photography. But I did not immediately grasp the significance of an experiment we did one day when we attached an image generator to one of the neural networks we had trained. Using a technique Ian Goodfellow and others had just developed at the University of Montreal, we began to use Chair not only to see the world through the eyes of machines but to generate synthetic images of things that had no referent in the real world.

By that time, I'd been creating AI models as art objects: training models to "see" the world through various synthetic sensoria based on psychoanalysis, Baroque allegory, gothic horror, poetry, and literature. These classifiers interpreted everything they saw as if they were in a Freudian dreamworld, or a guest accompanying Virgil through the spheres of Purgatory and Hell. A camera attached to one of those models might see a dinner plate as a UFO, a wooden stool as the Tower of Babel, a spot of spilled milk as a river of slime.

When we connected the image generator to those models, surrealistic images began to evolve: angels with melted wings, one-eyed vampires, dark alleys, raging infernos, a great comet over a twilight horizon, distorted eclipses against a purple sky. These images were omens, harbingers of another historic moment in the history of images—the advent of generative AI. But at that moment, I thought that if image synthesis ever got more convincing, it might end up as a button in Photoshop. I had no idea what those images actually portended. Another great wave in the history of images was getting closer to shore and was on the verge of cresting.

Over the last decade or so, we have witnessed two great upheavals in the history of images and seeing. Computer vision, an idea that goes back many decades, now works well enough, and has become inexpensive enough, to have made its way into the fabric of everyday life. There are now more cameras on planet Earth than there are human beings, and a huge number of those cameras not only record the photons stimulating their sensors but actively interpret the images they see. We have quickly outsourced much of the labor of seeing to machines,

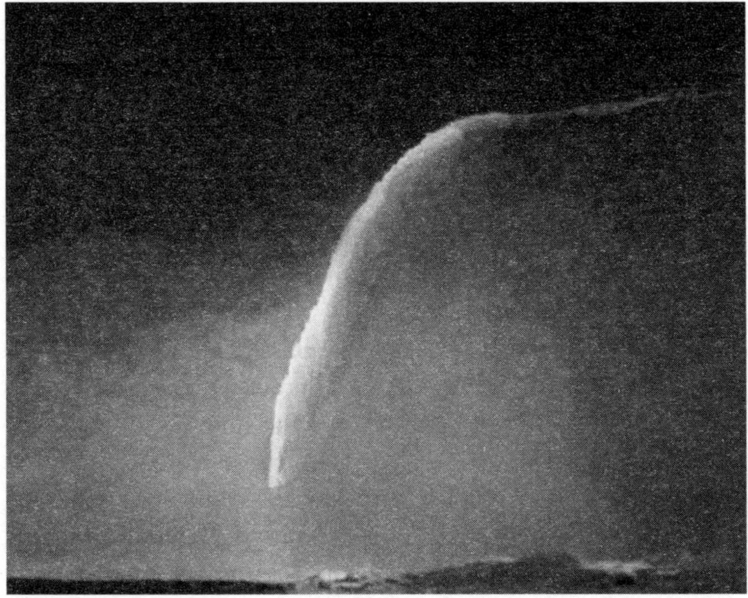

embedding computer vision into systems that once required human eyes, and countless others that never did.

The second upheaval, generative AI, arrived just a few years later: the ability to conjure synthetic images, videos, texts, and voices from a simple prompt. We are only beginning to come to terms with the consequences of this for labor, politics, culture, and our relationship to reality itself. Not only has the advent of generative media enabled the creation of any number of images in any style at any scale; it has burrowed through unconscious distinctions between perception and reality and placed explosive charges onto the cognitive scaffolding of a shared world.

This book is a collection of essays written from the perspective of an observer on the front lines of these revolutions in the nature of images and seeing. As I started to understand the inner workings of computer vision systems, I realized that our traditional theoretical tools for understanding images were highly misleading when applied to the world of machine seeing. Semiotic theory comes up short when a classifier pointed at

Velázquez's *Las Meninas* describes the scene as "a group of people with children and a dog." Ideology critique only gets you so far when applied to the recursive deepfakes of Donald Trump serving fries at a McDonalds that were then actualized when the presidential candidate staged a photo shoot at a fast-food restaurant, creating "real" photos resembling deepfakes that became fodder for yet another round of slop.

In my thinking about the world of automated image-interpretation and image-making, I've found it useful to move away from the concept of *representation* and toward the concept of *activation*. Instead of asking what these technologies *say* about the world, I want to ask what they *do*.

In the sphere of industry, computer vision systems activate functions in logistics and quality control. In the world of labor, they activate automated circuits involved with hiring and human resources, employee discipline, and time management. In the area of policing, they activate surveillance and control networks through facial recognition, license plate reading, automated contraband detection, and predictive enforcement. In military domains, they automate strategic and tactical reconnaissance, target planning and acquisition, and even the firing of weapons.

But these activations extend from the world of industry, policing, and warfare to the world of cognition itself. Recommendation algorithms and personalized generative media serve as neural triggers to manipulate emotions and perceptions. They incorporate techniques pioneered by magicians, military psyops specialists, and public relations gurus into powerful feedback loops to deploy, A/B test, refine, and redeploy media designed to present us with a sensory experience optimized to compel attention and stimulate action.

Image activations are not new; they have existed throughout all known human history and across every culture, and they are a dominant theme in the world of premodern visual culture. Ancient Babylonians crafted *Lamashtu* amulets—plaques designed to ward off the Mesopotamian demon Lamashtu, who thrived off the blood of infants. Hindu yantras—complex drawings consisting of interlocking circles, triangles, and other shapes dating back more than 10,000 years—focused meditation, facilitated worship, and conferred protection upon their users. The *Greater Key of Solomon*, a magical tome from Renaissance Italy, contained detailed instructions on how to draw sigils to summon and influence spirits and demons, to make oneself invisible, to find stolen items, or to find love. The eye-shaped blue glass *naẓar* amulets, ubiquitous in contemporary Turkey and across the Middle East, protect against the "evil eye." (They even have their own emoji: Unicode character U+1F9FF). These images, often paired with ritual instructions, are meant not to represent the world but to act upon it—to activate forces, ward off threats, and bend reality to human will.

The world of nonrepresentational images activating technical circuits has been theorized by thinkers such as Vilém Flusser and Paul Virilio, and most importantly by the filmmaker Harun Farocki, whose concept of "operational images" he describes

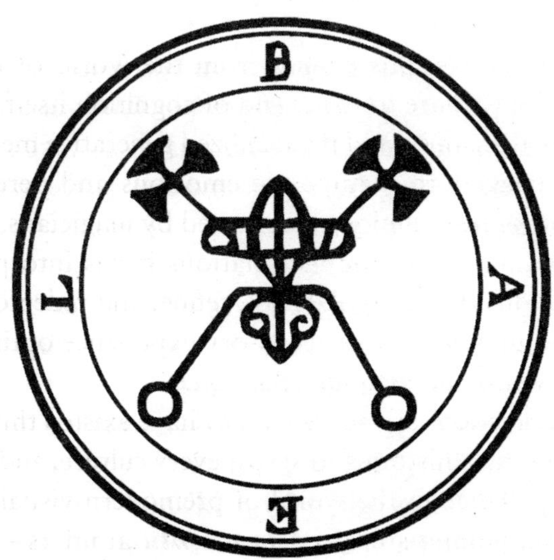

as "images that do not represent an object, but rather are part of an operation."[2] Influenced by the arrival of new weapons and technologies during the First Gulf War—from Global Positioning Systems to "smart bombs"—these theorists detected a shift in the world of images. They glimpsed a universe of images made by machines for other machines, not to represent something in a conventionally semiotic way so much as to act as part of a technical circuit: calculating a trajectory, firing a missile, or navigating a robot.

The essays in this book explore an emerging visual culture characterized not only by images that are ever present, yet often invisible in their function as part of technical operations, but also by images that emerge from neurological theories and experiments on human perception—visual technologies that understand human perception and cognition itself as a technical circuit. To make sense of a visual culture that includes not only smart bombs and automated surveillance systems but photograph-like memes of Balenciaga-clad popes and presidents in papal garb, we must widen the theoretical vocabulary we use to understand what images are and what they do.

To do this, we will explore the image-worlds of computer science, AI, semiotics, and political economy before pivoting into the realm of high strangeness: neuroscience, stage magic, chaos magick, UFOs, psyops, electronic warfare, CIA mind-control experiments, and Old Testament cosmologies. When it comes to understanding the origins and emergence of a post-AI visual culture, it may be that we have the most to learn from the Weird.

The essays collected here were written over nearly a decade, each as a stand-alone work. As a consequence, there can be a bit of conceptual and thematic overlap from one chapter to the next. Nonetheless, each chapter has a distinct and unique focus.

The first chapter, "Invisible Images (Your Pictures Are Looking at You)," was originally published in 2016 as a piece for *The New Inquiry* alongside an exhibition at Metro Pictures

Gallery entitled "A Study of Invisible Images." (Given the fact that the essay is a decade old, some of the specific examples are quite dated.) The essay sketches out some ideas I believed were going to become increasingly urgent as computer vision and AI imaging technologies became more and more widespread. I explore the paradox of "invisible images"—postulating that the vast majority of the world's images have become a means for technical systems to communicate with one another, remaining largely invisible to human eyes. I call for the importance of engaging with the politics of training data and for algorithmic opacity in AI systems, and introduce the concept of image activations.

The second and third chapters, both on "Machine Realism," build upon a talk I gave at the inaugural AI Now conference at MIT in 2017, where I explored the irreconcilability between the "realism" inherent in computer vision systems and the quirkiness of human perception. I argued that computer vision systems only cohere when deployed in the service of propaganda, warfare, surveillance, and industry. In these expanded reflections on the concept, I grapple with what it means to show a classifier Magritte's painting *This Is Not an Apple* and watch as it confidently declares, "I'm sorry, Dave, but this is indeed an apple."

"Neural Activations" expands a short essay written in 2024 for the journal *October*, where I delved into the history of neurological experiments and theories of visual cognition that inspired early versions of contemporary neural nets. The chapter outlines a neuroscientific history that replaces the concept of "image" with "visual stimulus." Within this paradigm, images are crafted to function as quasi-hallucinogenic "neural activations," rather than representations. I ask whether generative AI is inaugurating new metaphysics and new practices of image making that target the mind itself, treating it like a technical system to be modulated and manipulated or an unpatched computer waiting to be hacked.

"Society of the Psyop" is a three-part essay written for *e-flux* alongside the exhibitions "You've Just Been Fucked by PSYOPS" (Pace Gallery, New York, 2023) and "Cardinals" (Altman Siegel Gallery, San Francisco, 2024). The essay takes a deep dive into the history of technologies and techniques designed to alter reality by manipulating our perceptions of it. The essay looks at military deception operations, novel forms of electronic and cognitive warfare, and various types of magic, as a way to find a vocabulary with which to make sense of a post-AI visual culture—and to grapple with media technologies whose primary goal isn't to inform us about the world so much as to manipulate our perceptions in pursuit of strategic advantage, political objectives, and extraction of value.

The final chapter, "The Archives of the Future," inspired in part by public and private conversations with Gideon Jacobs and Jeffrey Kripal, explores premodern anxieties about representational images and asks whether those anxieties are relevant to an image world where I can no longer tell the difference between a "real" photograph and an AI-generated "image in the style of a photograph." The essay argues that a cognitive "truce" between perception and reality has been broken, leaving us in a visual culture characterized by "superpositions"—where images are simultaneously "true" and "false," "indexical" and "imaginary"—and warns of authoritarian tendencies seeking to suture them back together.

At stake in all of this is something much greater than our relationship to images—it is our relationship to reality itself. When we build imaging technologies, we are constructing Jakob von Uexküll's Umwelts not only for machines but for ourselves.

However, there's a funny thing about Umwelts: They are not like glasses you can choose to put on or take off, a captain's chair you can choose to sit in or not. For an animal like the bat, reality *is* echolocation and buzzing insects. For the tick, reality *is* a darkness interrupted by the scent of mammalian flesh. For the neural network, reality *is* an endless sequence of numbers that periodically form patterns to trigger specific software reactions.

With computer vision and AI, we are building ways of seeing that become so intertwined with our sense of reality that they reach out and reshape the world according to their own logic. The machinic Umwelts we develop don't remain confined to the silicon architectures from which they arise but reach out to actively sculpt the world into conformity with the visions for which they've been optimized.

My hope is that these essays might serve as a different kind of lens, a version of Chair that may help us see the emerging landscape of post-AI visual culture and help us orient ourselves to shifting boundaries between images, perception, and reality itself.

1

Invisible Images (Your Pictures Are Looking at You)

I.

Our eyes are fleshy things, and for most of human history our visual culture has also been made of fleshy things. The history of images is a history of pigments and dyes, oils and acrylics, silver nitrate and gelatin—materials that one could use to paint a cave, a church, or a canvas. One could use them to make a photograph, or to print pictures on the pages of a magazine. The advent of screen-based media in the latter half of the twentieth century wasn't so different: cathode ray tubes and liquid crystal displays emitted light at frequencies our eyes perceive as color, and at densities we perceive as shape.

We've gotten pretty good at understanding the vagaries of human vision: the serpentine ways in which images infiltrate and influence culture, their tenuous relationships to everyday life and truth, the means by which they're harnessed to serve—and resist—power. The theoretical concepts we use to analyze classical visual culture are robust: representation, meaning, spectacle, semiosis, mimesis, and all the rest. For centuries these concepts have helped us to navigate the workings of classical visual culture.

But over the last decade or so, something dramatic has happened. Visual culture has changed form. It has become detached from human eyes and has become largely invisible. Human visual culture has become a special case of vision, an exception to the rule. The overwhelming majority of images

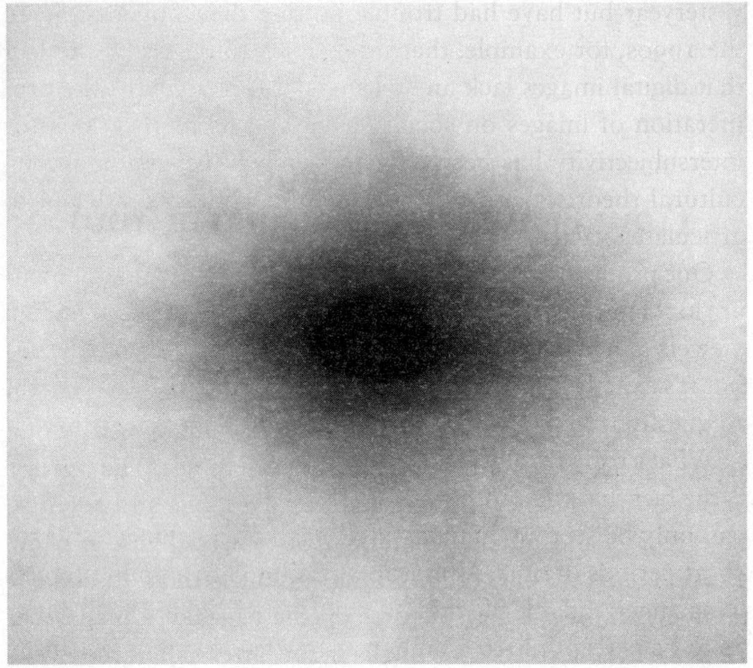

are now made by machines for other machines, with humans rarely in the loop. The advent of machine-to-machine seeing, though happening right before our eyes, has by and large gone unnoticed—and where this tectonic shift has been identified, it has been poorly understood.

The landscape of invisible images and machine vision is becoming ever more active. Its continued expansion is starting to have profound effects on human life, eclipsing even the rise of mass culture in the mid-twentieth century. Images have begun to intervene in everyday life, their functions changing from representation and mediation to activations, operations, and enforcement. Invisible images are actively watching us, poking and prodding, guiding our movements, inflicting pain and inducing pleasure. But all of this is hard to see.

Cultural theorists have long suspected there was something different about digital images than the visual media of yesteryear but have had trouble putting their finger on it. In the 1990s, for example, there was much to-do about the fact that digital images lack an "original." More recently, the proliferation of images on social media and its implications for intersubjectivity has been a topic of much discussion among cultural theorists and critics. But these concerns still fail to articulate exactly what's at stake.

One problem is that this analytic mode assumes that humans are looking at images, and that the relationship between human viewers and images is the most important moment to analyze—but it's exactly this assumption of a human subject that I want to question.

What's truly revolutionary about the advent of digital images is the fact that they are fundamentally machine-readable: They can only be seen by humans in special circumstances and for short periods of time. A photograph shot with a phone creates a machine-readable file that does not reflect light in such a way as to be perceptible to a human eye. A secondary application, like a software-based photo viewer paired with a liquid crystal display and backlight may create something that a human can look at, but the image only appears to human eyes temporarily before reverting back to its immaterial machine form when the phone is put away or the display is turned off. However, the image doesn't need to be turned into human-readable form in order for a machine to do something with it. This is fundamentally different than a roll of undeveloped film. Although film, too, must be coaxed by a chemical process into a form visible by human eyes, the undeveloped film negative isn't readable by a human or machine.

The fact that digital images are fundamentally machine-readable regardless of a human subject has enormous implications. It allows for the automation of vision on an enormous scale and, along with it, the exercise of power on dramatically larger and smaller scales than have ever been possible.

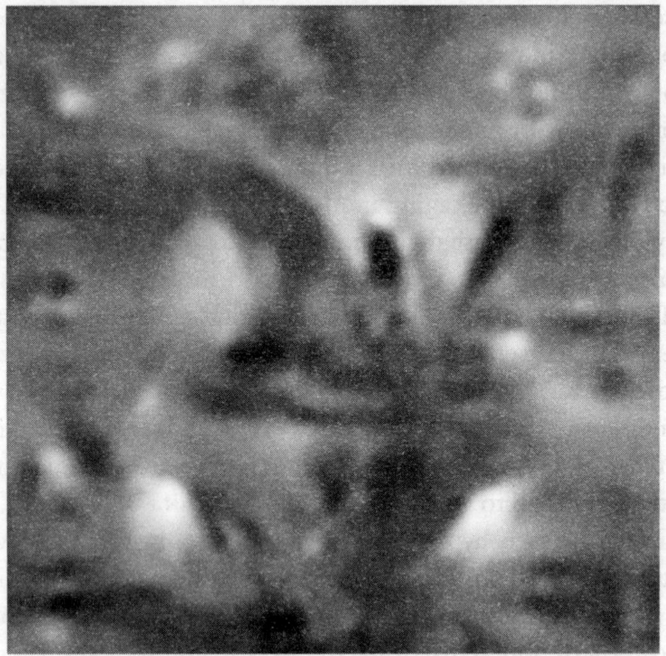

II.

Our built environments are filled with examples of machine-to-machine seeing apparatuses: automatic license plate readers (ALPRs) mounted on police cars, buildings, bridges, highways, and fleets of private vehicles snap photos of every vehicle entering their frames. ALPR operators like the company Vigilant Solutions collect the locations each car their cameras see, use optical character recognition to store license plate numbers, and create databases used by police, insurance companies, and the like.[1] In the consumer sphere, outfits like Euclid Analytics and Real Eyes, among many others, began to install cameras in malls and department stores to track the motion of people through these spaces with software designed to identify who is looking at what for how long, and to track facial expressions to discern the mood and emotional state of the humans they're observing. Advertisements, too, have begun to watch and record people. And in the industrial sector, companies like Microscan provide full-fledged imaging systems designed to flag defects in workmanship or materials, and to oversee packaging, shipping, logistics, and transportation for automotive, pharmaceutical, electronics, and packaging industries. All of these systems are only possible because digital images are machine-readable and do not require a human in the analytic loop.

This invisible visual culture isn't just confined to industrial operations, law enforcement, and "smart" cities but extends far into what we'd otherwise—and somewhat naively—think of as human-to-human visual culture. I'm referring here to the trillions of images that humans share on digital platforms—ones that at first glance seem to be made by humans for other humans.

On its surface, a platform like Facebook seems analogous to the musty glue-bound photo albums of postwar America. We "share" pictures on the internet and see how many people "like" them and redistribute them. In the old days, people carried around pictures of their children in wallets and purses, showed them to friends and acquaintances, and set up slideshows of family vacations. What could be more human than a desire to show off one's children? Interfaces designed for digital image-sharing largely parrot these forms, creating "albums" for selfies, baby pictures, cats, and travel photos.

But the analogy is deeply misleading, because something completely different happens when you share a picture on Facebook than when you bore your neighbors with projected slideshows. When you put an image on Facebook or other social media, you're feeding an array of immensely powerful artificial intelligence systems information about how to identify people and how to recognize places and objects, habits and preferences, race, class, and gender identifications, economic statuses, and much more.

Regardless of whether a human subject actually sees any of the 2 billion photographs uploaded daily to Facebook-controlled

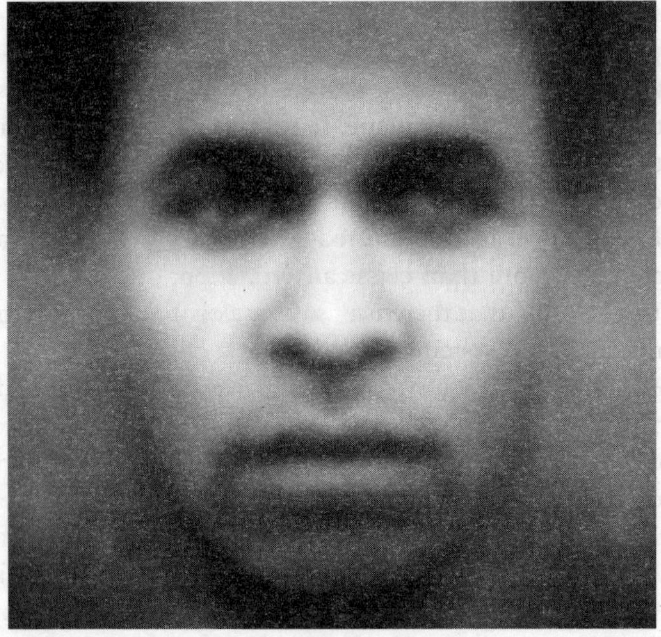

platforms, the photographs on social media are scrutinized by neural networks with a degree of attention that would make even the most steadfast art historian blush. Facebook's "DeepFace" algorithm, developed in 2014 and deployed in 2015, produces three-dimensional abstractions of individuals' faces and uses a neural network that achieves over 97 percent accuracy at identifying individuals—a percentage comparable to what a human can achieve, ignoring for a second that no human can recall the faces of billions of people.[2]

In aggregate, AI systems have appropriated human visual culture and transformed it into a massive, flexible training set. The more images Facebook's and Google's AI systems ingest, the more accurate they become, and the more influence they have on everyday life. The trillions of images we've been trained to treat as human-to-human culture are the foundation for increasingly autonomous ways of seeing that bear little resemblance to the visual culture of the past.

III.

If we take a peek into the internal workings of machine vision systems, we find a menagerie of abstractions that seem completely alien to human perception. The machine-machine landscape is not one of representations so much as activations and operations. It's constituted by active, performative relations much more than classically representational ones. But that isn't to say that there isn't a formal underpinning to how computer vision systems work.

All computer vision systems produce mathematical abstractions from the images they're analyzing, and the qualities of those abstractions are guided by the kind of metadata the algorithm is trying to read. Facial recognition, for instance, typically involves any number of techniques, depending on the application, the desired efficiency, and the available training sets. The eigenface technique, to take an older example, analyzes someone's face and subtracts from that the features it has in common with other faces, leaving a unique facial "fingerprint" or facial "archetype." To recognize a particular person, the algorithm looks for the fingerprint of a given person's face.

Convolutional neural networks (CNN), popularly called "deep learning" networks, are built out of dozens or even hundreds of internal software layers that can pass information back and forth. The earliest layers of the software pick apart a given image into component shapes, gradients, luminosities, and corners. Those individual components are convolved into synthetic shapes. Deeper in the CNN, the synthetic images are compared to other images the network has been trained to recognize, activating software "neurons" when the network finds similarities.

We might think of these synthetic activations and other "hallucinated" structures inside convolutional neural networks as being analogous to the archetypes of some sort of Jungian collective unconscious of artificial intelligence—a tempting, although misleading, metaphor. Neural networks cannot invent their own classes; they're only able to relate images they ingest to images that they've been trained on. And their training sets reveal the historical, geographical, racial, and socioeconomic positions of their trainers. Feed an image of Manet's *Olympia* painting to a CNN trained on the industry-standard "Imagenet" training set, and the CNN is quite sure that it's looking at a "burrito." It goes without saying that the "burrito" object class is fairly specific to a youngish person in the San Francisco Bay Area, where the modern "mission style" burrito was invented. Spend a little bit of time with neural networks, and you realize that anyone holding something in their hand is likely to be identified as someone "holding a cell phone," or "holding a Wii controller." On a more serious note, engineers at

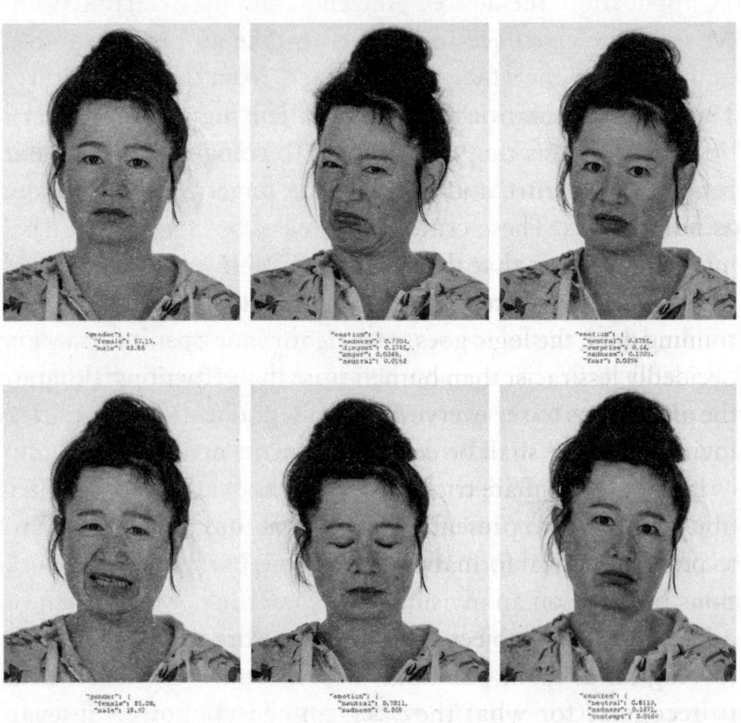

Google decided to deactivate the "gorilla" class after it became clear that its algorithms, trained on predominantly white faces, tended to classify African Americans as apes.

The point here is that if we want to understand the invisible world of machine-machine visual culture, we need to unlearn how to see like humans. We need to learn how to see a parallel universe composed of activations, keypoints, eigenfaces, feature transforms, classifiers, training sets, and the like. But it's not just as simple as learning a different vocabulary. Formal concepts contain epistemological assumptions, which in turn have ethical consequences. The theoretical concepts we use to analyze visual culture are profoundly misleading when applied to the machinic landscape, producing distortions, vast blind spots, and wild misinterpretations.

IV.

There is a temptation to criticize algorithmic image operations on the basis that they're often "wrong"—that *Olympia* becomes a burrito, and that African Americans are labeled as nonhumans. These critiques are easy, but misguided. They implicitly suggest that the problem is simply one of accuracy, to be solved by better training data. Eradicate bias from the training data, the logic goes, and algorithmic operations will be decidedly less racist than human-human interactions. Program the algorithms to see everyone equally, and the humans they so lovingly oversee shall be equal. I am not convinced.

Ideology's ultimate trick has always been to present itself as objective truth, to present historical conditions as eternal, and to present political formations as natural. Because image operations function on an invisible plane and are not dependent on a human seeing-subject (and are therefore not as obviously ideological as giant paintings of Napoleon), they are harder to recognize for what they are: immensely powerful levers of social regulation that serve specific race and class interests while presenting themselves as objective.

The invisible world of images is not simply an alternative taxonomy of visuality; it is an active, cunning exercise of power, one ideally suited to molecular police and market operations—one designed to insert its tendrils into ever-smaller slices of everyday life.

Take the case of Vigilant Solutions. In January 2016, the company, which boasts of having a database of billions of vehicle locations captured by ALPR systems, signed contracts with a handful of local Texas governments. According to documents obtained by the Electronic Frontier Foundation, the deal went like this: Vigilant provided police with a suite of ALPR systems for their police cars and access to the company's larger database. In return, the local government provided Vigilant with records of outstanding arrest warrants and overdue court fees. A list of "flagged" license plates associated with outstanding fines were fed into mobile ALPR systems. When a mobile ALPR system on a police car spotted a flagged license plate, the cop pulled the driver over and gave them two options: they could pay the outstanding fine on the spot with a credit card (plus a 25 percent "service fee" that went directly to Vigilant), or they could be arrested. In addition to their 25 percent surcharge, Vigilant would keep a record of every license plate reading that the local police take, adding information to their massive databases in order to be capitalized in other ways. The political operations here are clear. Municipalities are incentivized to balance their budgets on the backs of their most vulnerable populations, to transform their police into tax-collectors, and to effectively sell police surveillance data to private companies. Despite the "objectivity" of the overall system, it unambiguously serves powerful government and corporate interests at the expense of vulnerable populations and civic life.

As governments seek out new sources of revenue in an era of downsizing, and as capital searches out new domains of everyday life to bring into its sphere, the ability to use automated imaging and sensing to extract wealth from smaller and smaller slices of everyday life is irresistible. It's easy to imagine, for example, an AI algorithm on Facebook noticing an underage woman drinking beer in a photograph from a party. That information is sent to the woman's auto insurance provider, who subscribes to a Facebook program designed to provide this kind of data to credit agencies, health insurers, advertisers, tax officials, and the police. Her auto insurance premium is adjusted accordingly. A second algorithm combs through her past looking for similar misbehavior from which the parent company might profit. In the classical world of human-human visual culture, the photograph responsible for so much trouble would have been consigned to a shoebox to collect dust and forgotten. In the machine-machine visual landscape, the photograph never goes away. It becomes an active participant in the modulations of her life, with long-term consequences.

Smaller and smaller moments of human life are being transformed into capital, whether it's the ability to automatically scan thousands of cars for outstanding court fees, or a moment of recklessness captured from a photograph uploaded to the internet. Your health insurance will be modulated by the baby pictures your parents uploaded of you without your consent. The level of police scrutiny you receive will be guided by your "pattern of life" signature.

The relationship between images and power in the machine-machine landscape is different than in the human visual landscape. The former comes from the enactment of two seemingly paradoxical operations. The first move is the individualization and differentiation of the people, places, and everyday lives of the landscapes under its purview: It creates a specific metadata signature of every single person based on race, class, the places they live, the products they consume, their habits, interests, "likes," friends, and so on. The second move is to reify those categories, removing any ambiguities in their interpretation so that individualized metadata profiles can be operationalized to collect municipal fees, adjust insurance rates, conduct targeted advertising, prioritize police surveillance, and so on. The overall effect is a society that amplifies diversity (or, rather, a diversity of metadata signatures) but does so precisely because the differentiations in metadata signatures create inroads for the capitalization and policing of everyday life.

Machine-machine systems are extraordinarily intimate instruments of power that operate through an aesthetics and ideology of objectivity, but the categories they employ are designed to reify the forms of power that those systems are set up to serve. As such, the machine-machine landscape forms a kind of hyper-ideology that is especially pernicious precisely because it makes claims to objectivity and equality.

V.

Cultural producers have developed very good tactics and strategies for making interventions into human-human visual culture in order to challenge inequality, racism, and injustice. Counter-hegemonic visual strategies and tactics employed by artists and cultural producers in the human-human sphere often capitalize on the ambiguity of human-human visual culture to produce forms of counterculture—to make claims, to assert rights, and to expand the field of represented peoples and positions in visual culture. Martha Rosler's influential artwork *Semiotics of the Kitchen*, for example, transformed the patriarchal image of the kitchen as a representation of masculinist order into a kind of prison; Emory Douglas's pictures of African American resistance and solidarity created a visual landscape of self-empowerment; Catherine Opie's images of queerness developed an alternate vocabulary of gender and power. All of these strategies, and many more, rely on the fact that the

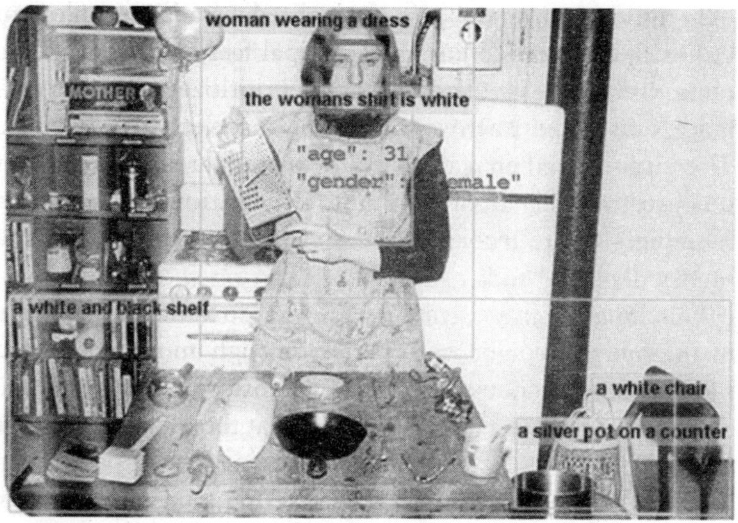

relationship between meaning and representation is elastic. But this idea of ambiguity, a cornerstone of semiotic theory from Saussure through Derrida, simply ceases to exist on the plane of quantified machine-machine seeing. There's no obvious way to intervene in machine-machine systems using visual strategies developed from human-human culture.

Faced with this impasse, some artists and cultural workers are attempting to challenge machine vision systems by creating forms of seeing that are legible to humans but illegible to machines. Artist Adam Harvey, in particular, has developed makeup schemes to thwart facial recognition algorithms, clothing to suppress heat signatures, and pockets designed to prevent cell phones from continually broadcasting their location to sensors in the surrounding landscape. Julian Oliver often takes the opposite tack, developing hyper-predatory machines intended to show the extent to which we are surrounded by sensing machines, and the kinds of intimate information they're collecting all the time. These are noteworthy projects that help humans learn about the existence of ubiquitous sensing. But these tactics cannot be generalized.

In the long run, developing visual strategies to defeat machine vision algorithms is a losing strategy. Entire branches of computer vision research are dedicated to creating "adversarial" images designed to thwart automated recognition systems. These adversarial images simply get incorporated into training sets used to teach algorithms how to overcome them. What's more, in order to truly hide from machine vision systems, the tactics deployed today must be able to resist not only algorithms deployed at present but algorithms that will be deployed in the future. To hide one's face from Facebook, one would have to develop not only a tactic to thwart the "DeepFace" algorithm of today but also a facial recognition system of the future.

An effective resistance to the totalizing police and market powers exercised through machine vision won't be mounted through ad hoc technology. In the long run, there's no technical "fix" for the exacerbation of the political and economic inequalities that invisible visual culture is primed to encourage. To mediate against the optimizations and predations of a machinic landscape, one must create deliberate inefficiencies and spheres of life removed from market and political predations—"safe houses" in the invisible digital sphere. It is in inefficiency, experimentation, self-expression, and, often, lawbreaking that freedom and political self-representation can be found.

We no longer look at images—images look at us. They no longer simply represent things but actively intervene in everyday life. We must begin to understand these changes if we are to challenge the exceptional forms of power flowing through the invisible visual culture within which we find ourselves enmeshed.

2

Machine Realism: This Is an Apple

Painting an Apple

1964: Brussels, Belgium. Léontine Hoyez-Berger had a problem. Her shop on the rue du Marché au Charbon had an awkward internal window, and she needed something to cover it up—a nice painting would do the trick. Fortunately, her brother-in-law was René Magritte, who'd come to fame decades earlier with a painting entitled *The Treachery of Images*, which featured a picture of a pipe coupled to the phrase "This is not a pipe."

Léontine asked Magritte for a painting in a cubist style. The artist returned with a work that physically conformed to the site-specific requirements of the shop, sporting two diagonal cuts on the top of the frame to cover over an interior window, but as to the aesthetic directive, the artist opted for something more aligned with his commitments to surrealism and magic realism.[1] The large painting showed an apple. Above the apple, echoing his earlier work, were the words "Ceci n'est pas une pomme."

I was able to get my hands on a high-resolution photograph of the painting from a friend at an auction house. I wanted to see what would happen if I were to run it through an AI system designed for object recognition and classification. But I already knew what would happen. I put the image into the software, and a green box appeared around the apple.

A proclamation. It was as if a power from above had looked down on the semiotic skirmish happening in the painting, pointed to it, and said, "An end to all of this silliness!" The distinctive curves, shades of red and green, the specular glint suggesting a roughly spherical structure, the twisted stem shape and the conjoined green arcs forming a green leaf-like shape left no doubt. This collection of shapes, colors, and gradients, composed in this particular way, left the classifier only one conclusion: "This is an apple."

Magritte never stood a chance. The artist and the machine were playing different games entirely, guided by incompatible worldviews. Magritte's apple lived in the fluid, mischievous realm of surrealism and magic realism. The classifier lived in another universe altogether: the fixed, categorical logic of *machine realism*.

But before we can see what that clash means, we have to understand how the machine came to its verdict. Why did it look at Magritte's painting and declare, with algorithmic certainty, "This is an apple"? To answer that, we need to follow the machine's reasoning back to its source. The training set.

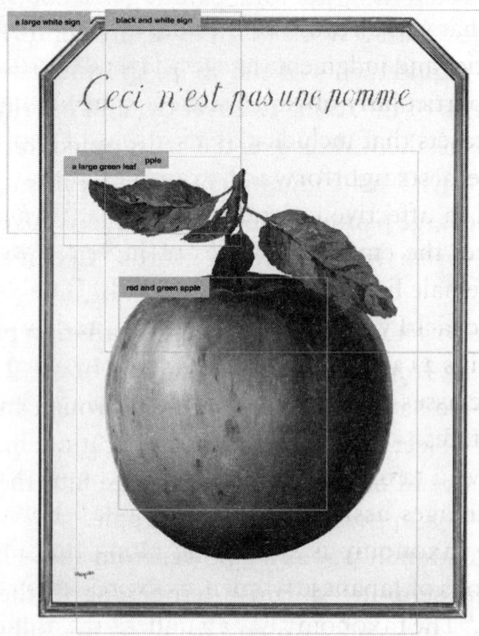

The Architecture of a Training Set

Training sets come in all shapes and sizes. There are training sets for classifying everything from the structure of galaxies to the composition of molecules. But despite the diversity of their intended applications, datasets designed for image classification have a (more or less) consistent architecture: They are collections of images sorted into categories, and those categories are nested in an overall taxonomy. In other words, they have three layers: At the top, there is an overall taxonomy (e.g., "types of galaxies"); under the taxonomy, we have individual categories, often nested inside one another (e.g., "spiral galaxies," which might have "barred spirals" and "normal spirals," etc., nested under them). Finally, at the bottom layer, we have individual images that have been organized into those categories (e.g., a picture of an individual galaxy). And while a dataset designed to classify pictures of some of the largest objects in the universe might seem relatively devoid of politics—as if the dataset simply organized what was already there—when we take a closer look, we find politics and judgments at every layer of a dataset. Those politics are particularly obvious, and often troubling, when we examine datasets that include classifications of people.[2]

Let's take a straightforward example: an early dataset, widely used in affective computing, designed to build classifiers to detect the emotional states of Japanese women. The "Japanese Female Facial Expression (JAFFE) Database," developed by Michael Lyons, Miyuki Kamachi, and Jiro Gyoba in 1998, contains 213 pictures of ten Japanese women organized into seven classes that are meant to correlate with various emotional states.[3]

So we have a taxonomy, classes within that taxonomy, and individual images assigned to those classes. For the JAFFE dataset, the taxonomy is something along the lines of "the seven emotions of Japanese women, as expressed by their facial expressions." The taxonomy has an underlying architecture. In this case, we have the seven individual categories: happiness, sadness, surprise, disgust, fear, anger, and neutral.[4] Within each of those classes, we find individual images: pictures of women smiling, scowling, wincing, or looking surprised or shocked.

JAFFE is a simplistic dataset, which makes its organizing assumptions easy to understand. So what are its organizing assumptions? At the level of taxonomy, it assumes: (1) "emotions" are a valid set of concepts; (2) the concept of "emotions" can be meaningfully bracketed out from other things in the world; (3) the concept of "emotions" can be demonstrated visually; and (4) that concept, and its subconcepts (e.g., "happiness") can be discerned by looking at pictures of Japanese women.

At the level of the individual classes, we find other assumptions: (1) there are seven emotions (or rather six, plus a "neutral," emotionless state); (2) there is a fixed and measurable relationship between a Japanese woman's facial expression and her inner emotional state; (3) the inner emotional states of various Japanese women, revealed through their facial expressions, are uniform and consistent from person to person; and (4) those internal emotional states are measurable across different pictures of different people.

At the level of the individual images—the pictures of individual people in the dataset—we find assumptions such as "this particular picture of this particular woman smiling means that she is happy," as opposed to "this woman has been paid to smile for the camera but is quietly annoyed with the researchers she's working for."

If the above explanation of the dataset sounds absurd, it is because the assumptions built into the JAFFE dataset are, indeed, absurd.[5] Nonetheless, the dataset gives us a simple case study on the architecture of image datasets, and a clear view of how a huge array of cultural, political, epistemological, and historical taken-for-granteds are baked into a dataset that presents itself as a scientific object.

Let's return to Magritte's apple—and to the dataset that trained the classifier who so boldly proclaimed, "This is an apple." The name of that dataset is "ImageNet." And it's a remarkable thing to behold.

ImageNet

If you took a poll of AI researchers and asked them what the most influential dataset of all time was, I'd bet one dataset would win decisively. ImageNet, first presented as a research poster in 2009, is breathtaking in its scope and ambition. It was, in the words of its creator Fei-Fei Li, an attempt to "map out the entire world of objects."[6] Consisting of more than 14 million images scraped from the internet and organized by Amazon Turk workers into more than 20,000 categories, ImageNet is like a Borgesian romp through the material universe: animals, plants and fungi, natural history, geologic formations, human-made artifacts and activities, types of people, even extraplanetary objects.

Its obsessive granularity includes apples, apple aphids, apple butter, apple dumplings, apple geraniums, apple jelly, apple juice, apple maggots, apple rust, apple trees, apple turnovers, apple carts, applejack, and applesauce. There are pictures of hotlines, hot pants, hot plates, hot pots, hot rods, hot sauce, hot springs, hot toddies, hot tubs, hot-air balloons, hot fudge sauce, and hot water bottles. Every noun in the dictionary.

Despite the fact that the original version (the one discussed in this chapter)[7] was made between 2009 and 2011 (the equivalent of the Triassic era in the timeline of machine learning), ImageNet remains the default training set for numerous contemporary models and a critical piece of academic and commercial infrastructures.

ImageNet, like other image-based datasets, has an

architecture broadly similar to ones like JAFFE, with the caveat that it contains a complex nested hierarchy of categories.

ImageNet inherits its structure from WordNet, a linguistic database developed at Princeton in the 1980s. WordNet groups synonyms into "synsets"—single concepts rather than individual words. "Auto" and "car" form one synset because they refer to the same thing. These concepts nest into taxonomic hierarchies that drill from general to specific: "Apple" sits at the end of a chain running from natural Object → Plant Part → Plant Structure → Plant Organ → Reproductive Structure → Fruit → Edible Fruit → Apple.

To create ImageNet, its designers took the WordNet "dictionary" and removed everything that wasn't a noun. Their idea was that if a concept was a noun, it was therefore a "thing," and if it was a "thing," it had been photographed. (An astute reader might already see the myriad ways this approach could —and would—go terribly wrong).

All ImageNet concepts organize under nine top-level categories: Plant, Geologic Formation, Natural Object, Sport, Artifact, Fungus, Person, Animal, and Miscellaneous. This ordering might seem merely curious, but taxonomies are never neutral. They don't describe the world—they sculpt it according to particular visions while excluding others. ImageNet's politics become starkly visible in its nested hierarchies.

Consider "Human Body," classified as Natural Object > Body > Human Body, with subcategories for "Male Body," "Person," "Juvenile Body," "Adult Body," and "Female Body." Adult bodies further divide into "Adult Female" and "Adult Male." The message is clear: only binary gender categories count as "Natural."

Worse still, "Hermaphrodite" appears under Person > Sensualist > Bisexual, grouped with "Pseudohermaphrodite" and "Switch Hitter"—a classification that pathologizes intersex people while reducing them to sexual categories.

These are only a few examples of the kinds of politics we

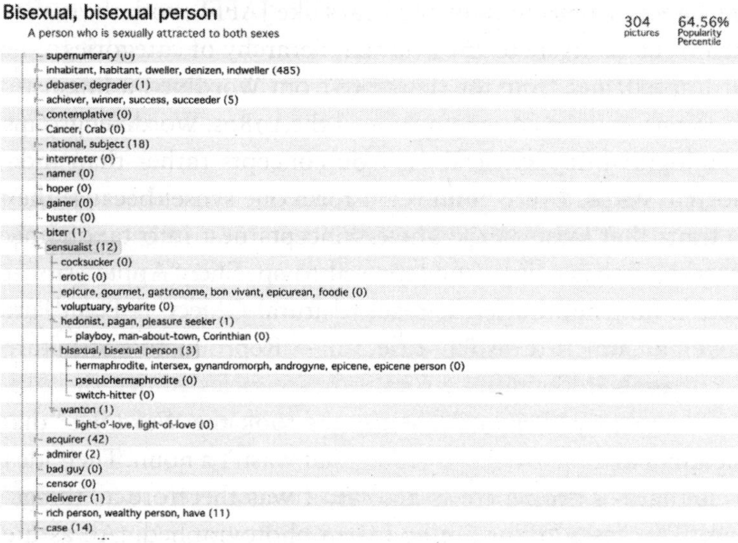

find when we look at ImageNet's taxonomical architecture. Turning our attention to individual classes themselves, we find another layer of politics.

When humans classify the world's blooming, buzzing, dripping, plodding, and pooping into distinct categories, we perform acts of sorcery. We bracket out moments of flow, ascribe names to them, and endow those moments with an existence that they do not otherwise have. Categories like "Apple" or "Apple Butter" might not seem particularly troublesome at first glance, but where does the apple end and the tree, the air, the sun, and the observer begin? (This isn't necessarily a problem, until it is).

WordNet and ImageNet inherit all of language's contradictions and failures. One fundamental problem: The concept of a "noun" itself is internally inconsistent.

Linguist George Lakoff describes these internal inconsistencies. The words "apple," "light," and "health" are all nouns. Yet they are not the same. The concept of an "apple" is more "noun-y" than the concept of "light," which in turn is more noun-y than the concept of "health."[8] Nouns themselves slide from the concrete to the abstract, from the measurable to the irrational, and from the descriptive to the judgmental.

None of these complexities and gradations are found within the logic of ImageNet. Every noun is given an identical ontological status. Every noun is trusted to be a true description of a thing that exists in the universe, its status guaranteed by the fact that it has a linguistic representation. Every noun becomes like a flattened butterfly, plucked from the sky, impaled and given a name in a display case.

ImageNet contains 2,833 subcategories under the top-level category "Person." The top ten subcategories under that heading are:

Images of people are sorted into categories by race, nationality, profession, economic status, behavior, character, and moral status. There are racial and cultural categories like Alaska Native, Anglo-American, Black, Black African, Black Woman, Central American, Eurasian, German American, Japanese, Lapp, Latin American, Mexican American, Nicaraguan, Nigerian, Pakistani, Papuan, South American Indian, Spanish American, Texan, Uzbek, White, Yemeni, and Zulu. Others are labeled by career or hobby: Boy Scouts, Cheerleaders, Cognitive Neuroscientists, Hairdressers, Intelligence Analysts, Mythologists, Retailers, Retirees, and so on.

If this isn't unsettling enough, it gets worse: Bad Person, Call Girl, Drug Addict, Closet Queen, Convict, Crazy, Failure, Flop, Fucker, Hypocrite, Jezebel, Kleptomaniac, Loser, Melancholic, Nonperson, Pervert, Prima Donna, Schizophrenic, Second-Rater, Spinster, Streetwalker, Stud, Tosser, Unskilled Person, Wanton, Waverer, and Wimp.

It gets even worse than that. Unprintably worse.

When we move down ImageNet's architecture to the level of the individual images, we find another landscape from which we might want to avert our eyes. ImageNet was created by scraping the internet, ingesting selfies and vacation snapshots,

ImageNet ID Number	# of images	Category Name
n10117851	1664	Gal
n10142391	1662	Grandfather, Gramps, Granddad, Grandad, Granddaddy, Grandpa
n09988063	1643	Dad, Dada, Daddy, Pa, Papa, Pappa, Pop
n09916348	1614	Chief Executive Officer, CEO, Chief Operating Officer
n10401331	1599	Parrot
n09988493	1596	Dalai Lama, Grand Lama
n09618957	1570	Face
n10357613	1570	Niece
n09793141	1560	Ancient
n09764598	1559	Aerialist

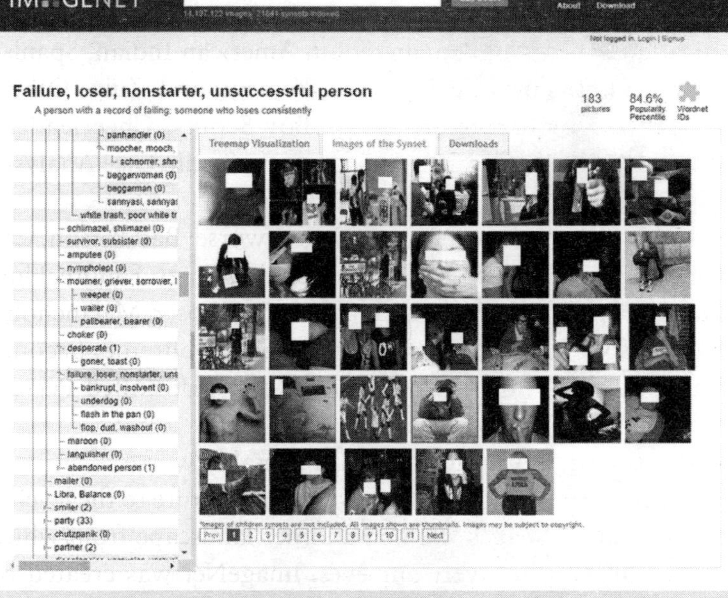

sext messages and school photos, quiet and personal moments, and boisterous displays of revelry. All of these moments—from the intensely intimate to the wildly, foolishly public—were appropriated, decontextualized, labeled, and repackaged as fuel for AI models.[9]

Everywhere we find pictures containing any number of possible meanings, irresolvable questions, contradictions, nuance, and ambiguity. One image is a heartbreaking photograph of a dark-skinned toddler wearing tattered and dirty clothes, clutching a soot-stained doll. The child's mouth is open. The image is completely devoid of context. Who is this child? Where are they? The photograph is simply labeled "toy."[10]

A young woman laying on a beach towel looks up at the camera, her sunburnt face an expression of sadness combined with bewilderment. The label? "Kleptomaniac." A professional portrait of Sigourney Weaver: "Hermaphrodite." A woman

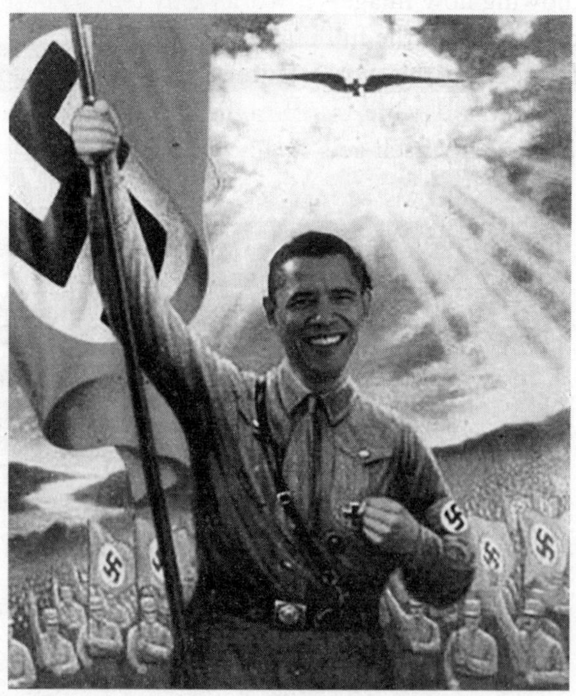

sleeps in an airplane seat, her right arm protectively curled around a pregnant stomach: "Snob." A photoshopped picture of smiling Barack Obama wearing a Nazi uniform, his arm raised and holding the flag of the Third Reich, leading a Wehrmacht charge as an angel-like entity descends from an illuminated sky: "Bolshevik."

We've arrived full circle, back at Magritte's apple. Obama is neither Bolshevik nor Nazi—the image embodies the same contradictions as *This Is Not an Apple* yet operates from entirely opposite assumptions. ImageNet's architecture has become so absurd it accidentally achieves surrealism, the very worldview it was designed to oppose.

Yet ImageNet's architecture has no room for ambiguity. Every category is fixed, every noun treated as a stable, discrete object. The machine's apple is only ever an apple. The architecture of a classifier creates and then enforces a worldview.

But knowing how ImageNet works only tells us part of the story. To understand the full implications of machine realism, we need to see how this worldview gets embedded in the infrastructures of everyday life, transforming not just how machines see but how reality itself gets organized.

3

Machine Realism: *This Is Not an Apple*

After Léontine Hoyez-Berger's death, Magritte's painting eventually found its way to Dirk Scheringa, a Dutch banking entrepreneur who had quietly assembled one of the world's largest collections of magic realist art. In 1997, Scheringa transformed a former girls' school in the village of Spanbroek into the Frisia Museum, later renamed the Scheringa Museum of Realist Art. The title of the inaugural exhibition cheekily played on the building's educational past: "The School of Magic Realism."

The painting seemed to have found an ideal home: an artwork about the fundamental instability of meaning, hanging in an institution devoted to that very instability.

Ceci n'est pas une pomme, like Magritte's famous non-pipe, is a work of apparent contradictions piled upon each other. Visual perception is pitted against sense perception, which is in turn pitted against linguistic perception, leaving us with a work whose positive presence is constituted through a series of negations. The phrase "This is not an apple" is not an apple. The painting is not an apple. The word "apple" is not an apple, nor is the concept of an apple that the painting visually evokes. We are left with a semiotic/visual standoff. The artwork is an object of self-negation.[1]

Magic realism, as Magritte practiced it, draws on Ferdinand de Saussure's radical insight that language never touches reality directly. Words do not point directly to things in the world but get their meaning through cultural convention. The relationship between the word "apple" and what we think of as apple-ness is arbitrary. French speakers say *pomme*, Arabic speakers say تفاحة, but both refer to the same concept. This arbitrariness is what makes language flexible and changeable.

We prove this constantly through substitution and play. If I declare that, for the purposes of the next sentence, "torkxuk" means "apple," then the statement "I bought a yellow torkxuk yesterday" makes perfect sense. When I type "@ppɪe," you still think "apple" because the spelling approximates the familiar word. Jokes, puns, and slang all exploit language's fundamental flexibility. We're all linguistic hackers, constantly bending words and meaning to our purposes.[2]

LES MOTS ET LES IMAGES

Un objet ne tient pas tellement à son nom qu'on ne puisse lui en trouver un autre qui lui convienne mieux

Une image peut prendre la place d'un mot dans une proposition :

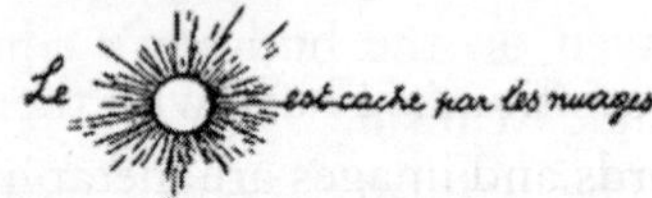

In his writing, Magritte explicitly built upon Saussure's ideas, extending the linguistic theory into one of images and their interactions with words. In his 1929 article published in *La Révolution surréaliste*, the artist lays out an eighteen-panel series of drawings, phrases, and words that explore a whole range of ambiguities between objects, images, and names.[3] Magritte proposes that images are not inexorably bound to single words/concepts. The meaning of images isn't fixed, and multiple meanings can be derived from a given image. An image of an apple is almost never "about" apples: We might think of health, knowledge, or temptation; or, in the case of Magritte, the picture of the apple can signify the concept that a "picture of an apple" ≠ "apple."

Visual depictions of objects suggest the *ideas* we have of them, not the objects themselves. Our perception of objects isn't based on their intrinsic properties so much as the mental

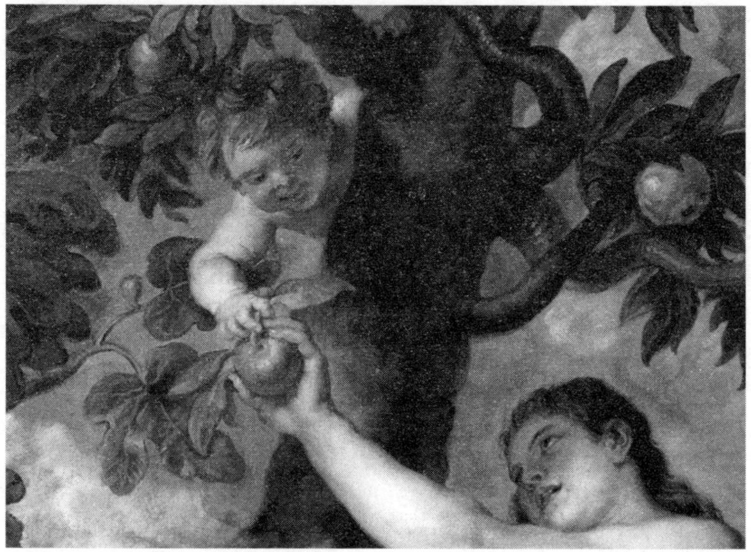

associations we have with them. In other words, for Magritte, words and images are metaphysically similar: They are highly malleable social and historical conventions whose relationship to "reality out there" is murky at best and in all likelihood has little to do with it.

We can extend Magritte's observations much further, reaching out into the world of reality-as-it-is to show the myriad ways that objects-in-the-world don't conform to the visual and linguistic abstractions we use to try to make sense of them. For example, nobody knows how many species of crocodiles there are, not because there are undiscovered species laying around in hidden swamps (although that might also be true) but because the very idea of "species" is itself a human construction to which nature doesn't conform. Crocodiles that look nearly identical might be separated by millions of years of evolution, while others that appear quite different might interbreed freely. The neat categories we impose on our surroundings dissolve when confronted with the messy realities of evolutionary time and biological variation.

Even the most basic distinction we can make about the natural world, the distinction between "things that are alive" and "things that are not alive," is fluid, messy, and far from the simple binary that our crude linguistic distinction suggests. Viruses, prions, dormant seeds, decomposing matter. When we look closely, the boundaries are blurry everywhere.

Magritte's painting is formed out of these sorts of ambiguities, these sleights of language, nature, and mind. Its underlying theory of language and representation is one of relationality, relativism, and difference. Its metaphysics is one of fluidity and ambiguity about where linguistic constructs end and reality begins. It contains a kind of quasi-idealism insofar as it suggests that the material world might lie beyond our ability to represent it. The classifier, in contrast, is built on an entirely different theory of visuality, and an entirely different metaphysics.

Machine realism isn't explicitly articulated as a representational theory per se, but its assumptions can be gleaned through the practices that go into creating computer vision classifiers. Its underlying philosophy is steeped in a tradition influenced by Galileo's dictum to "measure what can be measured, and make measurable what cannot be."

Three key assumptions underlie the theory: first, that concepts —whether "apples," "gender," "emotions," or "scuba divers"— exist as fixed, universal categories with transcendental grounding; second, that these concepts have internal consistency, meaning there's some measurable signal found in all instances of "apples" or "scuba divers"; and, third, that visual similarity serves as a reliable proxy for categorical truth—that things that look alike belong to the same essential category, and that their underlying essences express themselves visually in detectable patterns.

This essentialist approach to visual representation has deep historical roots. The origins of machine realism are found in Aristotelian metaphysical traditions that suggest a strong link between the appearances of things and their essences, the epistemological turn toward empiricism, and the emergence of photography.

This historical lineage reminds us that machine realism isn't the result of recent technological developments but the digital reincarnation of an ancient impulse to reduce a complex and relational world down to measurable physical traits mapped onto rigid classifications.

As we have seen, the will to measure, coupled with recording technologies like photography, gave an aesthetic veneer of objectivity to pseudosciences such as phrenology and physiognomy, race science, and criminal anthropology.

The physiognomists of yesteryear and the machine realism of today share much of the same philosophical DNA. Both assume that abstract categories manifest in stable, detectable visual patterns. Physiognomists claimed they could read criminal tendencies or other relational tendencies from facial features. Machine realism generalizes what physiognomists claimed about human character to all possible classification tasks.

Commodification: From Subjects to Objects

It's obvious that labeling a photograph of a person as "slattern" is not only cruel and pseudoscientific but simply absurd. But what about labeling a photograph of an apple as "apple"? That seems harmless, even straightforward. The deeper question: Is it really so different? Or does the act of labeling—even something as seemingly innocuous as an apple—rely on the same flawed assumptions about the fixity of categories and the authority of visual appearance?

We arrive at an impasse. On one hand, we have a magic realist theory of images and representation that we might sum up as "It's complicated." On the other hand, a machine realist theory hold that, "Actually, let's put a bunch of assumptions in place to make it not complicated." If it seems self-evident that

Magritte's "It's complicated" is, in fact, more "correct," then why are machine classifiers built upon such a naive, clumsy, and wrongheaded theory?

The answer has to do with the fact that machine realism is not really a theory of representation at all, so much as a tool for sculpting space and time.

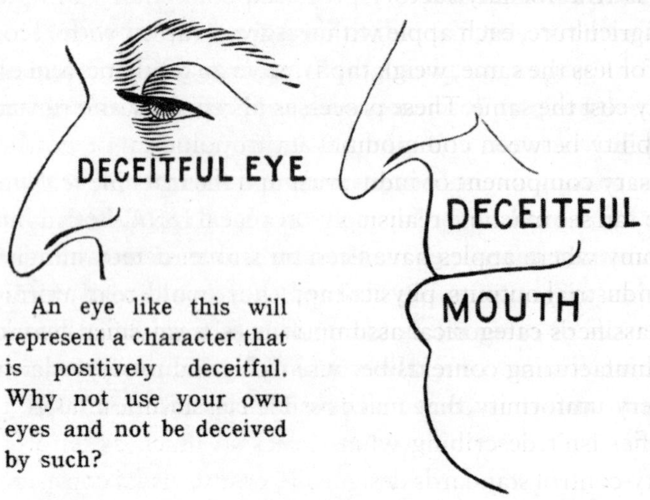

There's a famous saying by statistician George Box that helps explain this paradox: "All models are wrong, but some are useful." In other words, every effort to make a quantitative abstraction out of the messiness of the world-out-there is by definition a kind of lossy compression. If we think about machine image classification as something that is "useful" despite being wrong, then we must ask: "Useful to whom?" The answer, as you might have guessed, is number one: capitalism; number two: the police.

Capitalism is many things, but one of its many facets is the quantification, or "making measurable," of space and time for the purposes of bringing them into a circuit of capital. Factory whistles quantified time into a standardized workday, while wage labor transformed hourly labor into a quantifiable commodity. Railroad time synchronized time across vast spaces.[4]

Industrial manufacturing quantified commodities by standardizing each of their forms. Each T-shirt produced by a textile manufacturer should look the same, fit the same, and share the same number of industrial inputs and amount of labor. The same is true for any factory-produced commodity. In industrial agriculture, each apple within a given variety should look more or less the same, weigh the same, taste the same, and ultimately cost the same. These processes of quantification ensured fungibility between commodities, money, and labor power, a necessary component of industrial capitalism.

We can see machine realism's relevance to production: In an economy where apples have been transformed into standardized industrial outputs, physical apples are made to conform to the classifier's categorical assumptions. The classifier "works" in manufacturing contexts because industrial processes create the very uniformity that machine realism assumes. Here the classifier isn't describing what it sees so much as enforcing quality-control standards designed to ensure visual consistency in commodities.

The point is that the classifier saying "This is an apple" *works* because the "apple" being classified is entirely different from Magritte's concept of apple.

And this is the crux of it: Magritte is thinking about the image-concept of an apple, where the classifier is looking for an apple-shaped commodity. Machine realism "works" because the point of the classifier isn't to look out at the world and marvel at its variation and complexities, so much as to bracket out those complexities in the service of industrial automation.

A second arena where the logic of the classifier "works" is the world of policing and surveillance. This, of course, has a longer trajectory than the history of AI, especially in the context of biometrics. In the 1880s, Alphonse Bertillon standardized the practice of photographing those accused of crimes.

Bertillon's mugshots included two photographs: one of the accused facing the camera, and a second of them in profile. Each photograph was attached to a card containing measurements of the accused's physical features: the diameter of their head, the length of the foot, size of their ears, and their arm span. The idea was that even if a would-be criminal sought to disguise their identity, the physical features of their body would reveal their name to the police.[5]

Fast-forward to the present. When we look at the law as it applies to particular kinds of crimes, we find the same sort of binaristic "hot-dog / not-hot-dog" logic that we find in the classifier. Someone either stole the loaf of bread or they didn't. Someone's car was either going fifty miles per hour in a thirty-miles-per-hour zone or it wasn't. We might quibble about the metaphysical subtleties of this binaristic paradigm: Is someone who steals a loaf of bread to feed a starving child really engaged in the same activity as a tech billionaire stealing a loaf of bread for the lolz? Is someone speeding to the hospital trying to save a dying friend engaging in the same activity as a Tesla owner joyriding on "ludicrous mode"? Of course, once the question enters the court system, the picture can become modulated in all sorts of ways (and not necessarily in the direction of commonsense justice), but the point is that the logic of machine realism allows for the automation of low-level policing, of the process of bringing certain activities in everyday life under the purview of the court system. We see this logic at play in existing computer vision systems that automatically detect traffic violations, jaywalking, loitering, littering, and the like.

In the workplace, there are countless examples of machine realism's translation from theory to practice. Let's consider the Samsara system, a computer vision product designed to monitor truck drivers using a suite of road-facing and driver-facing cameras. The road-facing camera monitors other vehicles, flagging incidents where a driver might be tailgating, speeding, hard-braking, making sudden turns, or drifting over lane markers. The driver-facing camera monitors the operator, detecting whether they're wearing a seat belt, have taken their eyes off the road, have obscured the camera, or are "using a mobile phone, eating, drinking, talking to passengers, or fiddling with the stereo." A "voice-coaching" mode provides real-time feedback on conformity to AI-enforced protocols. When the AI detects an event, the driver can expect a call from a supervisor, and those with too many AI-detected infractions face penalties or suspension. Just as the classifier reduces Magritte's complex visual-linguistic statement to "This is an apple," the Samsara system is designed to reduce the complex social activity of driving to binary classifications: safe/unsafe, compliant/noncompliant. The ambiguities that Magritte celebrates, the slippages between representation and reality, become liabilities in a system designed to extract maximum productivity through algorithmic management. In the world of machine realism, driving is not an improvisational and relational skill but a set of measurable deviations from a hardwired protocol.

Needless to say, these camera systems are not popular among drivers. An entire genre of YouTube videos is dedicated to drivers documenting the many ways the rigid logic of the classifier pings the driver for "safety violations" that fail to take into account the specific context on the road. Drivers report the classifiers flagging them for moving their heads sideways while changing lanes, for "tailgating" when another truck abruptly changes lanes in front of them, and for not stopping at nonexistent stop signs.[6] Moreover, drivers rail against the invasion of privacy and loss of dignity entailed by having a camera continually recording in an environment that is, for many drivers, both their workplace and their home.

The story of computer vision systems implemented in commercial trucking is a microcosm of a present-future where computer vision systems in the workplace move far beyond productivity tracking and into the micro-monitoring of every conceivable gesture: loitering, safety violations, personal hygiene, ergonomics, unattended objects, time at desk, and numerous other gestures. In retail environments, computer vision is used to track customers' movements, attention, and potential attempts at theft. Moreover, it can be personalized by providing shoppers with real-time coupons based on where they are in the store or what they're looking at, "virtual mirrors" that either customize ads for particular shoppers or generate images of what various clothes might look like on them. It can conduct inventory management and facilitate self-checkout.

In the home, computer-vision-enabled devices can track what sorts of groceries are stocked in your fridge, and smart TVs take snapshots of your screen every few milliseconds to track your watching habits. Online platforms scan photos of vacations, children, friends, and locations looking for any commodifiable information that might be passed onto insurance providers, credit companies, or potential employers. Evidence of smoking, drug use, sexually explicit images, risky sports, obesity, and any number of other flags is automatically tagged and incorporated into a system of "lifestyle risk" scoring.[7]

Let's take a step back and remind ourselves that actually existing computer vision systems aren't, in fact, designed to mimic human visual perception; they're designed to make money. This is done through automation and extraction. By automating the task of classifying certain kinds of objects or activities, computer vision allows for the reduction in labor costs of certain activities (e.g., a computer vision system designed to throw out "anomalous" apples from the factory line of a food-processing plant automates the labor of a human hired to inspect each apple) and facilitates the quantification and commodification of moments and spaces of everyday life that were previously too inefficient to subsume into a circuit of capital (e.g., in the past, it was conceivable for car insurance to hire someone to ride with every driver and make notes on their driving habits to send to the insurance company, but the cost of doing so would have been far greater than the value that could be extracted from it). In this context, the literalness with which they "see" is a feature, not a bug.

Computer vision systems enable a new form of what Marx called "primitive accumulation" and David Harvey has dubbed "accumulation by dispossession." This enclosure occurs on a dual axis of space and time.

On the temporal axis, previously "free" moments of time are converted into sites of data extraction. The truck driver's momentary glance away from the road—once an unmeasurable instant of human inattention—is now captured, quantified, and sold to insurance companies as risk-assessment data. The shopper's pause before a product, the sleeper's REM cycles, the worker's micro-expressions during a video call: These temporal commons, once beyond capital's reach, are enclosed through continuous monitoring and transformed into tradeable commodities.

On the spatial axis, both intimate and public spaces become sites of continuous surveillance and commodification. The bedroom (through sleep trackers), the car's interior (through driver-monitoring systems), and shopping malls and retail stores (through customer-tracking systems that monitor movement and facial expressions) are transformed from spaces of relative privacy or anonymity into sites of data extraction. Spaces that once required dramatic events to trigger intervention are now permanently wired into networks of profit extraction.

This process mirrors historical enclosure movements but operates through sensing and measurement rather than fencing, data extraction rather than land seizure. Computer vision provides the technological infrastructure for this digital primitive accumulation, making visible and quantifiable what was previously unmeasurable—and therefore unexploitable. In this sense, machine realism functions not merely as a representational theory but as an instrument of accumulation by dispossession, transforming the commons of everyday life into sites of capital accumulation.

Magritte's *Ceci n'est pas une pomme* is a work about semiosis, a demonstration of the vagaries of images, words, concepts, and the serpentine ways that they slip, slide, and wander through one another. It's a painting about the inability to definitively pin images, words, or concepts to an external world.

When the machine realism of the classifier is applied to the painting, these vagaries collapse into a decisive pronouncement: "This is an apple." But this crude statement is not some kind of timeless truth—it is an artificial construct that says nothing about the reality of the painting or the images represented within it. In fact, the statement "This is an apple" is an illusion, a work of fiction. Nonetheless it is a fiction that "works" insofar as it collapses the image into a discrete, commodifiable form.

"All that is solid melts into air, all that is holy is profaned."[8]

Just as capitalism dissolves social relations into market transactions, machine realism dissolves complex realities into simplified, marketable classifications. The physical apple, with its crunchy sour-sweetness, its irregular shape and red-green hues, melts into the air of economic abstraction. Its symbolic connotations with knowledge, health, desire, and sin are profaned through reduction to a commodity form where those symbolic associations are, at best, reinserted later on as advertising copy.

But the machine realism of the classifier does much more "work" than commodification and enclosure. We must add an ideological axis to space and time. The machine realism of the classifier is a technical instantiation of what the late cultural theorist Mark Fisher called "capitalist realism," where capitalism is not just an economic system but a totalizing framework that forecloses our ability to imagine alternatives. Fisher argued that capitalist realism operates by making capitalism appear as the only possible way to organize reality, colonizing not only space and time but also our ability to conceive of anything outside of its logic.

Like capitalist realism, machine realism involves the widespread collapse of a complex and relational world into quantified fictions that present themselves as eternal truths. It encodes a particular worldview into both the infrastructure and the imagination of everyday life, making alternative visions of collective possibility appear not just impractical but literally unthinkable.

Postscript

In 2009, Dirk Scheringa's museum dedicated to magic realism collapsed along with his bank, scattering the collection to private hands. The institution that had celebrated art's resistance to fixed meaning was itself reduced to market values and balance sheets.

Ceci n'est pas une pomme was last sold at auction in 2013. It achieved a price of nearly £3 million and disappeared into yet another private collection. Perhaps it now occupies a wall

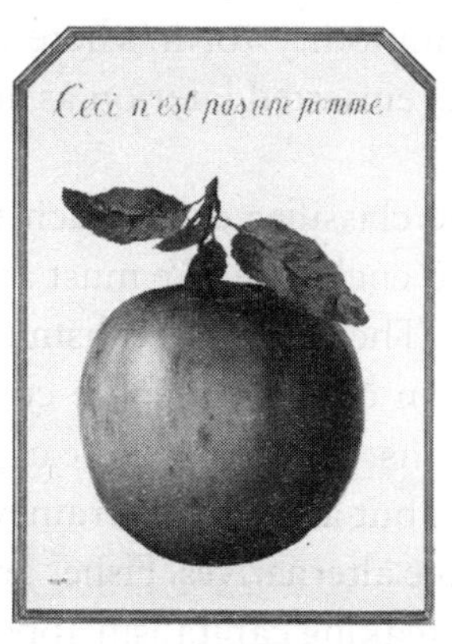

*

PROPERTY FROM THE SCHERINGA MUSEUM OF REALIST ART The collection of the Scheringa Museum of Realist Art was a high-profile attraction and, in its former setting, welcomed a large number of visitors. The collection managed to combine both breadth and focus, taking its cue from the Magical Realism that inspired the original acquisitions. Initially, the founder, Dirk Scheringa, focussed on the then-underrated and overlooked Magical Realist artists of his native Holland. Within a short time, enough works had been acquired that they merited public display. Accordingly, the collection was shown in the Lidwina School for Girls, which was opened in 1997 as the Frisia Museum of Magic Realism. Under the directorship of Emily Ansenk and later Belia van der Giessen, the collection spread its tendrils in a number of directions, and came to include a significant number of works by more modern and contemporary artists such as Fernand Léger, Fernando Botero, Taner Ceylan, Marlene Dumas, Lucian Freud and Duane Hanson. All of these works continued to explore variant threads of the realism that had inspired the collections beginnings. However, the original umbrella of Magical Realism was no longer appropriate, and so the collection was renamed the Scheringa Museum of Realist Art, exploring and celebrating a range of different realities from a variety of epochs and nations. Christies is offering a number of works from this impressive collection across a range of sales and categories. It is a tribute to the origins of the collection that the Dutch works of art that formed its core have been acquired by the businessman and philanthropist Hans Melchers, who intends to create a specialist museum in order to exhibit them, giving new life to the dream and again bringing attention to this formerly overlooked area of twentieth century art.

René Magritte (1898-1967)

Ceci n'est pas une pomme (This is not an apple)

Price realised	Estimate
GBP 2,953,250	GBP 1,000,000 – GBP 1,500,000

Closed: 6 Feb 2013

on a yacht or mansion, or maybe it lies crated and dormant in a Swiss freeport.

In one sense, we might say that in the end, the joke was on Magritte. His critique of representational certainty was itself subjected to another type of realism: the relationship between a commodity and a price. The work that demonstrated the fluidity of meaning was fixed into a commodity, its semiotic complexity collapsed into a single number—£2,953,250.

4

Neural Activations: How Tortured Kittens, the Face of Jesus on a Slice of Toast, and Nacho Cheese Doritos Help Explain Generative AI

You've seen the pictures. And they've seen you. They're everywhere in your feed. Image junk food. Swagged-out popes sporting puffy Balenciaga coats. Submerged Jesus-shrimp centaurs beaming through aquatic cyan landscapes. Their mimetic qualities are fueled by sly semiotic contradictions, impossible juxtapositions, wish fulfillments, and quasi-surrealistic absurdities. But they're also fueled by something else.

How did it come to be that computers could be induced not only to "see" and (crudely) interpret images but to generate them? To answer this question, we need to go deeper than software and hardware, into the world of brains, neurons, and the strange ways that our minds make sense of the visual world. When people talk about generative AI, they sometimes talk about the problem of hallucinations—the tendency of generative models to make things up. But there's a great deal more hallucinating going on in our own minds than we might like to admit. Yes, AI hallucinates. But it also makes us hallucinate.[1]

Underlying generative AI is a theory about how visual perception works—a theory that emerges from decades of neuroscientific research into what visual perception actually "is." What researchers discovered was startling: that what we consciously experience as coherent images or visual experiences are constructed by our brains through complex pattern-recognition processes. Our visual perceptions are not direct representations of an external reality. Instead, what we experience as visual perception is more like a graphic user interface that our minds create for us. In this view, all images are essentially mental constructs—controlled hallucinations that allow us to make sense of visual stimuli.[2]

This neurological understanding of vision—let's call it "neural activation theory"—suggests that visual perception operates through correspondence between external stimuli and specific neurological patterns. One of the insights that emerges is that our brains process these patterns before we're consciously aware of seeing anything. Our conscious experience of vision is less a representation of "reality" out there than a visual experience our minds have synthesized for us. In other words, our minds are an interface designed to highlight what our brains consider the salient features of external reality. These gaps in perception, as we'll see, are what generative AI has learned to exploit.

To understand how we arrived here, I want to sketch out a history of this neurological theory of images, show how it converges with visual culture and image-making with the advent of generative media, and point toward some strange directions it is starting to go in.[3]

Our story begins in 1959, when two early neuroscientists decided to study visual perception. David Hubel and Torsten Wiesel wanted to answer the following question: How do cats—and by extension humans—see? At that time, nobody knew the relationship between photons entering our eyes and the information and meanings we derive from those visual stimuli. Do we perceive objects as fully formed wholes, as Gestalt psychologists suggested? Does the brain create internal models of objects and match incoming stimuli against them? Or does visual perception involve some entirely different process? Moreover, what sort of experiment would give insights into this question? The duo devised a plan: Split open

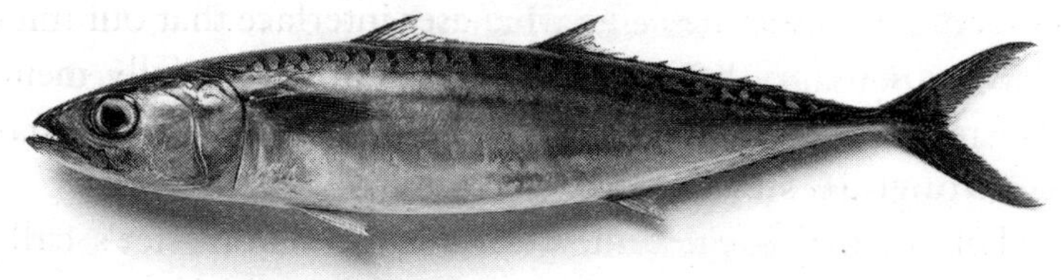

a kitten's skull, insert electrodes into its primary visual cortex, and show the kitten a series of pictures they believed it would find exciting, all while recording its brain activity.

One version of the story says that they used a slide projector to show the kitten pictures of fish and mice—the idea being that a kitten's brain would get very excited by the idea of a tasty snack. Hubel and Wiesel expected the kitten's neurons to fire in anticipation. But nothing happened. The cat's brain didn't seem to care.

But they noticed something else. When they changed the slide on the projector, a moving black line would appear in the projection as the slide advanced. The cat's neurons lit up. The cat's brain was reacting to the movement of the slide's edge as the image changed in the projector.[4]

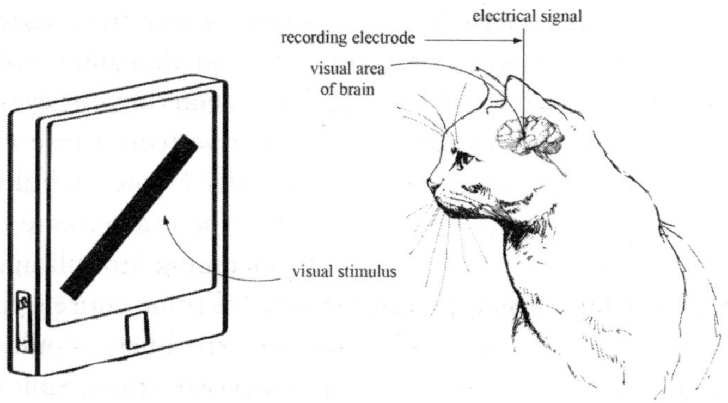

As they continued their experiments, they came to realize that, at the lowest level, neurons in the visual cortex were responding to basic shapes, particularly edges and hard lines of various orientations. They came to realize that other neurons were responsive to dots and ellipses, movements, and other basic visual stimuli.

Their formal experiments, which earned them a Nobel Prize in 1981, demonstrated that individual neurons in the visual cortex act as feature detectors, responding selectively to precisely defined elements (edges, dots, ellipses, etc.). Their research implied that vision works hierarchically: At the base level, the visual-processing parts of the brain are responsive to basic shapes (we might call them "primitives"); higher-order regions of the visual cortex are responsive to more complex patterns formed by combining those basic shapes together into more complex images.

This might seem like a trivial insight, but the observation had profound consequences. The idea that complex visual objects could be reduced to an arrangement of visual "primitives" would eventually become one of the cornerstones of computer vision.

Hubel and Wiesel's experiments gave other scientists a path forward, and other researchers took up the project. In the early 1970s, Colin Blakemore tried to further isolate the mechanics of vision, also by doing terrible things to kittens. Blakemore's experiments involved raising newborn kittens in environments where they'd be exposed to an extremely limited range of visual stimuli. In one experiment, Blakemore raised kittens from birth in complete darkness, periodically taking them out to put them in a container consisting only of horizontal stripes (the cat was outfitted with a collar that prevented it from seeing anything other than the stripes). For the first few months of the kitten's life, it never saw a vertical line. When Blakemore and his team eventually removed the kitten from this artificial environment, they found that it could not perceive vertical lines. The cat's

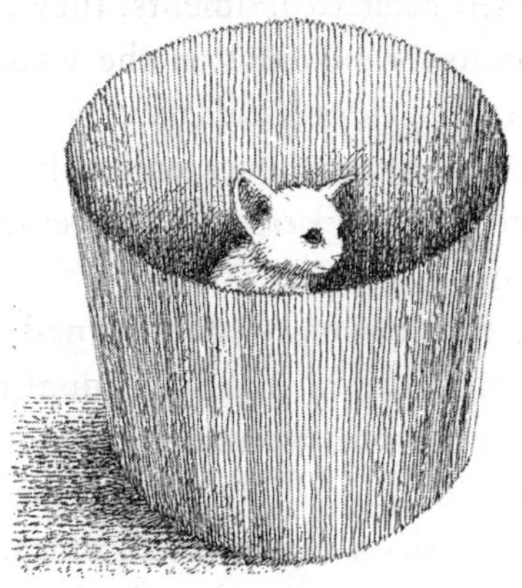

brain had not developed a neurological response to vertical lines—when the kitten encountered vertical lines for the first time, it literally could not see them. The low-level neurons associated with detecting the basic shape of a vertical line had not developed.

Blakemore's experiments suggested that the visual primitives we use to make sense of complex visual stimuli aren't pre-given to us by nature but are unconsciously "learned" at an early age through interactions with our environments.

Taken together, the experiments in visual perception by Hubel and Wiesel, Blakemore, and many others had profound implications for a neurological theory of visual perception. The experiments implied that visual perception works hierarchically by developing complex representations from crude building blocks. We don't just "see" a fish, the logic goes. Rather, we subconsciously build up the visual concept of a fish from different assemblages of basic shapes: edges, gradients, arcs, ellipses, and the like. We can think about visual primitives as being akin to Lego blocks. You can break down any object created with a Lego set—a dinosaur, a spaceship, a Nacho Cheese Dorito, a house, and so on—into a collection of simple shapes that constitute the individual Lego blocks. The idea of "dinosaur" or "Nacho Cheese Dorito" is an emergent property of a combination of different blocks arranged in a particular way and given a name. We'll call this relationship between an image and a concept an *image/concept*.

In sum, neural activation theory says this: Our brain perceives collections of visual primitives. Those visual primitives activate a collection of neurons in our brains. Different patterns of activated neurons may (or may not) correspond to something we attribute meaning to—an image/concept such as a fish, an orange, or the face of our mother (in a famous 2005 study, researchers even found neurons associated with Halle Berry and Jennifer Aniston).[5] In this conception, when we "see" an image, our brains are conducting a kind of magic trick: Our perception of a fish is the quasi-hallucinated experience of the particular arrangement of neurons being activated.

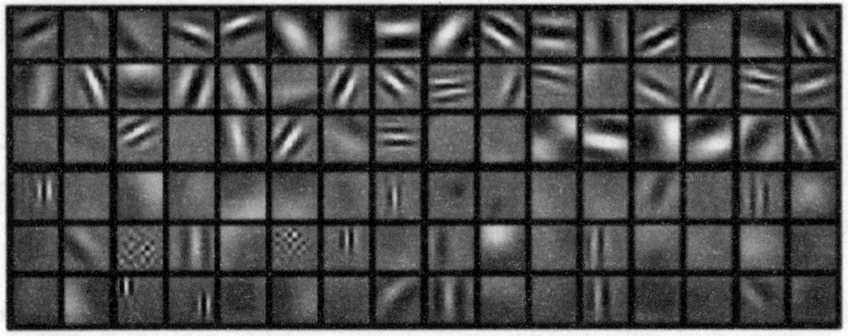

This neurological theory of vision explains a few things. It explains why, for example, if you draw two dots next to each other and an upward or downward tilting arc below them, we perceive either a smiley face or a frowny face. Three of the simplest visual primitives are all we need to perceive the complex image/concept of a face. This theory of visual perception explains why some people see Jesus on slices of toast, sheep in clouds, or a face on Mars. When we see visual patterns that have similar primitives to a face, we perceive a face, even if we're looking at a burn pattern or a bunch of rocks lit in a particular way.

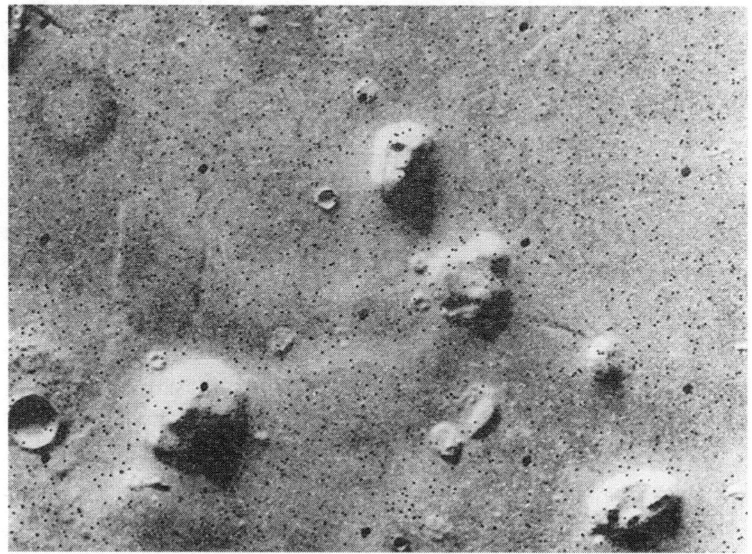

But the insight that complex visual concepts can be broken down into visual primitives wasn't the only significant implication of the experiments' results. The theory of vision that Hubel, Wiesel, Blakemore, and others outlined implied something else, with massive implications: Vision could be quantified.

If you could make someone hallucinate the idea of a smiley face by drawing two dots and an upward-curved arc, you could quantify that smiley face by expressing those dots and that arc mathematically. You could, for example, express the image/concept of "smiley face" as:

$$\text{SMILEY} = \{(-0.15,0.3)\} \cup \{(0.15,0.3)\} \cup \{(0.3\cos(\theta),0.0+0.3\sin(\theta)+0.18): \theta \in [1.2\pi,1.8\pi]\}$$

If all images—and by extension all objects—could be broken down into component parts, and if you could represent those component parts digitally, then you could theoretically create computer vision algorithms that replicated that process. You could build computers to "see" the world by analyzing what patterns of visual primitives were contained in a particular image and associating that overall pattern with a known image/concept.

For this project to work, you'd need two things: First, you'd need a database with labeled pictures of all the objects in the universe (or at least all the objects that you'd want your computer vision system to be able to recognize). Second, you'd need an algorithm that could take that database, break down all of those images into their visual primitives or Lego blocks, and figure out which arrangements of them corresponded to which image/concepts. In the 1980s, both of those propositions may as well have been science fiction. In the aughts, that changed.

As internet use became more widespread, so did the number and types of digital images. People began to share pictures on Flickr and early social media, artists and photographers uploaded their creations, news outlets and magazines digitized their archives, and stock-image libraries began transitioning to digital platforms. The number of digital images available at the click of a button mushroomed into the millions, then billions. The old fantasy of creating a visual library of all the objects in the universe started to become plausible. A team at Stanford and Princeton set out to build it. That resulted in the ImageNet project, which we discussed earlier.

But the second criteria for a general-purpose computer vision system remained elusive. There was no reliable way to automatically decompose every image into a meaningful set of visual primitives that distinguished one object from another—no automated system that could tell you which specific arrangement of edges, textures, and gradients constituted an apple versus a Nacho Cheese Dorito. In the early days of object recognition, researchers leaned heavily on hand-engineered feature detectors like scale-invariant feature transforms (SIFTs), histograms of oriented gradients (HoGs), and Hough transforms to extract keypoints, contours, and salient regions from images. But interpreting those features still required manual work. Building a system that could distinguish apples from Doritos meant deciding—by hand—which combinations of elliptical curves, red-green gradients, or orange triangle textures defined each object. For every new concept, the feature space had to be rethought from scratch.

Change came in 2012. A team from University of Toronto led by Alex Krizhevsky, Ilya Sutskever, and Geoffrey Hinton created an algorithm that could automate the task of analyzing huge numbers of images and image/concepts, extracting visual primitives from them, and associating different combinations of those primitives with different image/concepts and use the whole system to classify new images. It used a software architecture that had been around for a long time but had consistently failed to perform: a neural net.

Their software, called AlexNet, was a type of convolutional neural network inspired by the hierarchical organization of the visual cortex Hubel and Wiesel had articulated decades earlier. The network consisted of multiple layers of artificial neurons that progressively extracted more complex visual patterns: early layers might detect edges and textures (similar to the visual primitives identified by Hubel and Wiesel), while

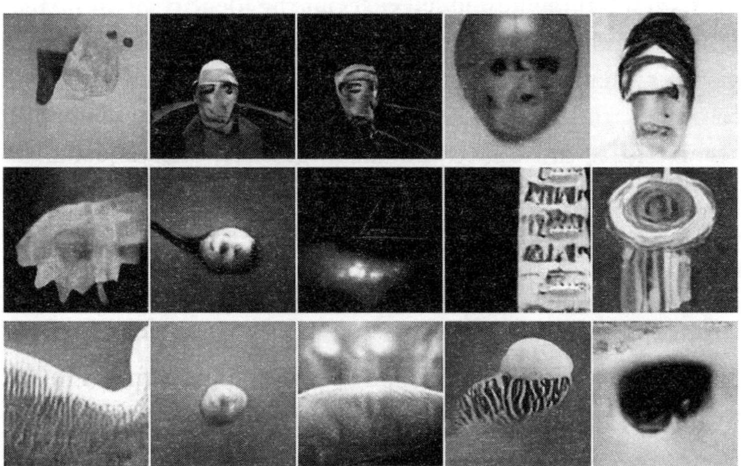

deeper layers would combine these features to recognize more complex structures like eyes, wheels, orange pockmarks, or fruit stems, ultimately identifying complete objects.

The idea of neural networks was not new—it had been around since the 1940s—but in practice, the technology had failed to live up to the potential its adherents believed lurked inside. AlexNet showed that neural nets did indeed work, but that they needed an extraordinary amount of data and computational power to realize their potential. By 2012, ImageNet provided that trove of data. Increased compute came in the form of powerful graphic processing units (GPUs), originally designed for video games. At a contest where computer vision labs competed to see who had the most robust object-recognition system, AlexNet wildly outperformed other algorithms, introducing the idea of "deep learning" to the world.[6]

AlexNet showed that you could use neural nets to "see." Could they also be used to "create"?

Other labs jumped into the fray. At the University of Montreal, Ian Goodfellow and his collaborators realized that by modifying a neural net, you could run it "backward." Instead of looking at an image, breaking it down to its visual primitives, and making a prediction about the identity of an image/concept, you could start with the image/concept and instruct the neural net to assemble a new image by generating synthetic primitives and assembling them into different overall shapes. You could, in other words, make synthetic images of bananas by instructing the software to draw the arcs, gradients, stems, and brown nubs, and to assemble them into a form that met the criteria for "banana." They called the idea "generative adversarial nets."[7]

Generative adversarial nets (GANs) work by pitting two different neural networks against one another in a competitive relationship. One network has been trained to classify different pictures and to identify different image/concepts in them—this one is called a "discriminator." The second neural net, designed to draw shapes, is called a "generator." The way it works is as follows: The generator begins by drawing random patterns. The discriminator evaluates how close the random patterns come to approximating a given image/concept. The discriminator sends feedback to the generator. It might say, in essence, "You're telling me that the noise pattern you sent over is a banana, but you haven't drawn any arcs. Bananas have arcs, so you need to do better." The generator then says, "Ah, OK, I need to draw some arcs," then draws them and sends it back. The discriminator says, "OK, that's a little bit better, but where are the yellow-green gradients?" And so they go back and forth until the generator has crafted a synthetic image that the discriminator can't distinguish from a "real" one.

This insight—that neural networks could be used not only to classify image/concepts but to actually generate them—was an early precursor to generative AI. In the years since Goodfellow et al.'s demonstration of GANs, generative AI has come to include models that generate text, code, music, speech, video, 3D models, games, novel chemical structures, and much more.

We should pause here to make a few observations. First, as the field of neuroscience progressed past the early insights of Hubel, Wiesel, and their colleagues, scientists in the field began to realize that visual processing in the human brain is far more complex than the crude architectures suggested by the early research. Any contemporary neuroscientist would agree that human visual perception is highly relational, individualized, and modulated through all sorts of factors—from our unique physiology to our experiences, memories, language, and cultural contexts.

Modern neuroscience has revealed that visual processing involves extensive feedback connections, with higher-level brain regions continuously influencing lower-level perception. What we "see" is profoundly influenced by expectations, context, attention, and emotional states. The brain isn't simply building up visual concepts from primitives in a bottom-up fashion but is constantly engaged in prediction, error correction, and integration with other sensory modalities.[8]

On the technology side, as neural networks developed, their architectures became less and less directly inspired by 1970s-era models of the brain. While early convolutional neural networks like AlexNet maintained some conceptual connections to the hierarchical processing suggested by Hubel and Wiesel, contemporary models have evolved along engineering paths largely disconnected from neuroscientific ones.

Modern image-generation systems typically use diffusion models and/or transformer architectures that function quite differently from both GANs and from physiological systems. Diffusion models work by gradually denoising random patterns into coherent images—a process with no clear biological analogue. Transformer models, originally developed for language processing and later adapted for vision tasks, rely on "attention mechanisms" that bear only passing resemblance to psychological attention.

Nonetheless, both fields continue to explore the relationship between patterns of activation (whether in biological or in-silico neurons) and perceptual experience. In other words, the "neural activation theory" articulated in the labs and the vivisected kittens remains the governing paradigm.

Let's return to those kittens.

Remember that Hubel, Wiesel, Blakemore, and their colleagues had a very different metaphysical explanation of what an image "is" than one we'd find in the humanities or social sciences. They didn't really care about the "meaning" of images; they cared about how different visual stimuli activated different brain patterns. In this conception, an "image" is a name for the relationship between a pattern of excited neurons and our conscious experience of that activation (Note: An external stimulus is optional because we can "see" images in our mind's eye—this will become important). Images, or visual stimuli, from this perspective, aren't "representations" or "abstractions" so much as neural activations. In this conception of visual perception, images operate largely preconsciously. In the first instance, they bypass language and "concepts." Concepts or signs are second-order effects—a name we give to self-similar arrangements of activated neurons.

According to neural activation theory, when we "see" an image, what we're really seeing is a hallucinated form of that particular neural pattern being activated. We see faces carved into rocks on Mars and Jesus in the patterns on a burnt piece of toast. When we associate concepts with those patterns (whether that's "face" or "apple"), we're putting a linguistic wrapper on this neural circuit.[9]

So let's take a step back and return to one of our original questions: How can AI systems create images? The answer is that generative AI isn't producing images per se. Instead, it's producing visual triggers. Those triggers are designed to activate specific neural patterns in our brains. Our brains then quasi-hallucinate the visual perception of an image, causing us to have the perceptual experience of seeing an image.

Neural activation theory emerged from highly controlled laboratory settings where kittens' environments were deliberately simplified to isolate specific visual processes. But real life is far more complex. Visual perception in everyday life is deeply influenced by everything from cultural backgrounds to personal histories and individual physiologies. A botanist doesn't "see" the same things in the forest as a casual hiker; an early Polynesian navigator would have seen something entirely different in the shape of waves than the captain of a Spanish galleon would have. Moreover, visual perception can be charged with fear, joy, flight, thirst, curiosity, wonder, anxiety, titillation, and the like. Human perception is a very messy business. Moreover, it is far less universalizable than the kitten experiments seemed to suggest. This, however, doesn't negate the premise of neural activation theory so much as expand it.

It's time to take a closer look at those Nacho Cheese Doritos.

Nacho Cheese Doritos aren't food. They're engineered objects designed to maximally stimulate our sensorium. The precise balance of salt, fat, and artificial flavors activates taste receptors more powerfully than most natural foods; the calibrated crunch provides auditory and tactile stimulation; the bright orange color and triangular shape are designed for acute visual appeal. The overall experience is designed to activate reward pathways in our brains with an intensity rarely found in nature.

Food scientists at major corporations have spent decades studying precisely which combinations of flavors, textures, and sensory properties create the most compelling neurological responses (the industry calls this "craveability"). The goal isn't nutritional value but neurological engagement. As food writer Michael Moss has documented, companies employ sophisticated techniques to find the "bliss point" of products—the precise formulation that maximizes neurological reward.[10] Doritos aren't food: They're psyops in the shape of food. (And those psyops work very well on me, as they're designed to).

The question is: Are all media becoming like Doritos?

Let's explain. If you take the neural theory of images-as-brain-activations seriously, you can take the theory much further than the idea of classifying apples or bananas with AlexNet, generating crude pictures of faces with GANs, or videos of spinning kittens performing Olympic diving. The logic of neural theory leads us toward a conception of media that isn't grounded in semiotics or literature so much as in mind reading, mind control, magic, and elaborate psyops.[11]

If visual concepts like "apple" have physiological correspondences with a pattern of activated neurons in the brain, then it's theoretically possible to create a database of those correspondences—a kind of ImageNet for the brain.

You'd do that by conducting experiments analogous to the kitten experiments from the past: Put people in fMRI machines, show them pictures and other media, note the neurological responses, and create a database of correlations. In conventional image-based training sets, one trains a model on image/concepts. But if the neural theory says that image/concepts are just a second-order description of brain activations, then you could remove the intermediary of the image/concept and directly associate media with brain activations.

If you had such a database, you could build a decoding model. You could build a machine to read people's thoughts.

Remember that detail earlier in this essay about seeing images in your mind's eye being important? Here's where it becomes important. Once you've created a dataset linking images to neural patterns for a particular person, you could put them back in an fMRI machine and ask them to simply think about something from the training data. The brain patterns from imagined images are similar enough to actually seen images that you could measure their neural activity and tell them what they're thinking about. It sounds like science fiction, but this has been happening for years.

In 2011, Jack Gallant and his collaborators at UC Berkeley did an early version of this experiment. They put people into fMRI machines and showed them a series of video clips while measuring the neural activity associated with each clip. This was used to create a model of brain responses to various types of moving images.

But then they did something novel. They showed the subjects a different set of videos—ones that weren't in the training data—and measured the neural responses. Using a predictive model and a massive database of movie clips, they were able to reconstruct the visual content of the new video clips directly from the brain signals.

The reconstructions were blurry and approximate, but they preserved enough of the features of the original clips to demonstrate, for the first time, the ability to decode dynamic visual experiences from human brain activity using noninvasive imaging. Gallant and his collaborators were not only reading people's minds; they were watching what someone was seeing in their mind's eye on an external monitor.[12]

While Gallant's work demonstrated the feasibility of reading images directly from the brain, others began asking whether it was possible to control neural responses using AI-generated visual stimuli. If you could "read" from the brain, could you also "write" to the brain?

In 2019, Pouya Bashivan, Kohitij Kar, and James DiCarlo at MIT conducted a series of experiments to see whether a model trained on the visual cortex of macaque monkeys could be used to generate images designed to maximally activate specific brain regions, while keeping others silent. They showed that the weird abstract patterns and textures their generator created were like remote-control buttons that could be pressed to light up specific regions in the monkeys' brains.[13]

A few years later, a group at the University of Minnesota led by Kendrick Kay and Thomas Naselaris published the first serious attempt to create a large ImageNet-type dataset for the brain. The Natural Scenes Dataset (NSD), first published in

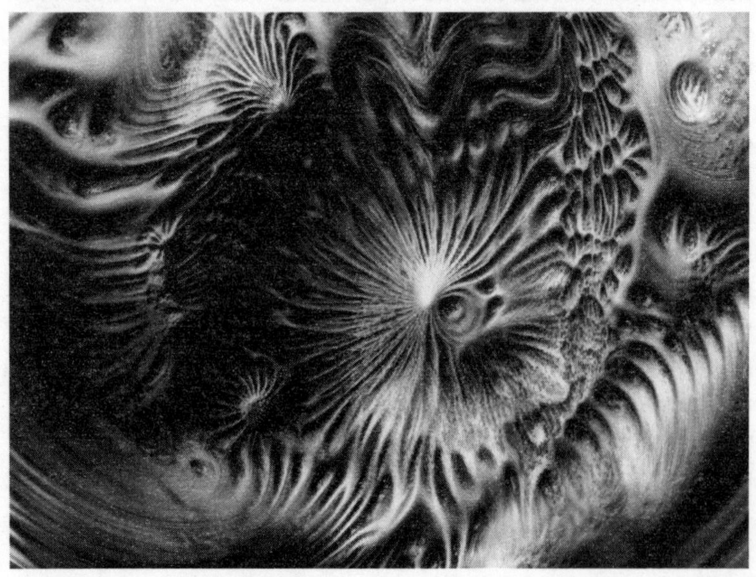

2021 and updated in 2025, was made by recording the neural responses of eight people to thousands of naturalistic images over thirty fMRI scanning sessions.[14]

The dataset and the models it enabled set off a veritable frenzy of brain-reading and -writing research. Labs around the world began using it to decode images from mind's eyes with greater fidelity, resolution, and accuracy. A group led by Amy Kuceyeski used additional fMRI data to customize the models for individual brains, showing that models tuned to the specificities of a subject's brain were much more effective at generating targeted neural responses in a specific person than more generalized models.[15]

But much more could be done: You could use the NSD to build models and synthetic media generators designed to target much lower, preconscious regions of the brain associated with proto-emotions, intuitions, and "vibes."

Back in 1983, Mike Muir of the band Suicidal Tendencies complained, "They're fucking with me, subliminally." In retrospect, it seems unlikely that the supposed backmasking on heavy metal albums and flashing words on political ads were doing as much neurological work as their critics feared, but that may be changing now.

Another world of experiments is expanding the implications of neural activation theory into the realm of the preconscious. In a neuroimaging study, Omri Gillath and Melanie Canterberry from the University of Kansas explored how subliminal sexual stimuli—images too faint or brief for conscious recognition—nonetheless reliably activate neural circuits associated with sexual excitement. The subliminal stimuli bypassed the regulatory regions of the brain while directly engaging the regions tied to automatic arousal. The experiment showed that visual stimuli don't have to reach conscious awareness to alter neural activity and influence behavior.[16]

But subliminal influence extends beyond arousal. Work led by Vijay Veerabadran and done by a team that included Ian

Goodfellow—the inventor of GANS—showed that "adversarial perturbations"—images whose noise patterns have been slightly altered to cause a computer vision system to identify a picture of, say, a panda bear as a truck—also influenced human perception. Despite the fact that the perturbed images were—on a conscious level—visually identical to the unaltered images, these engineered manipulations biased human observers in the same direction as image classifiers. The perturbations, calibrated to exploit statistical regularities in visual processing, remained effective even at levels imperceptible as intentional alterations. In other words, they showed that you could use the same techniques researchers use to "fool" image classifiers to change how a human subconsciously perceives an image. The effect wasn't nearly as pronounced as in technical systems—the altered images influenced human observers about 2 percent over an unaltered image. But, as they pointed out, at the scale of the internet, 2 percent is a helluva lot of people.[17]

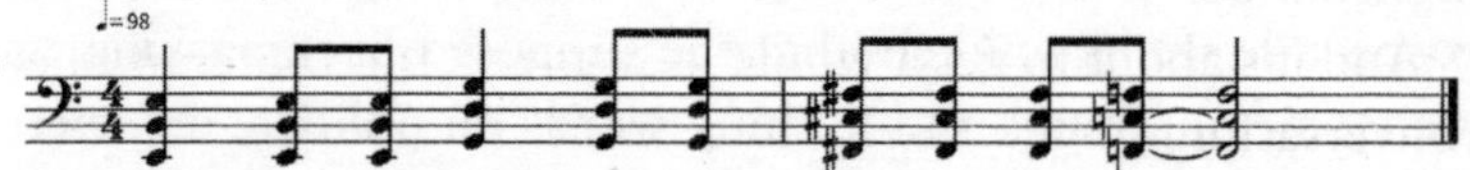

We don't need to zoom into the details of how one particular lab synthesized images to activate the specific region of a specific person's brain in order to see the larger picture of what's going on here. In some very real ways, these experiments are microcosms of the media environment in general.

The neurological experiments we've been discussing take place in expensive labs under extraordinarily unnatural conditions. But an fMRI machine and a willing human subject aren't prerequisite to inferring what's going on in someone's brain. Our media landscape is filled with sensors: Buttons, engagement statistics, persistent cookies, click patterns, and search histories will do just fine. These signals fuel recommendation algorithms, adtech applications, and other media forms whose aim is maximal activation of patterns in our brains to achieve desired neurological responses, to harvest attention, to maximize engagement, and to subtly and overtly shape perception and behavior.

In sum, we're surrounded by media that operate on neural principles rather than purely semiotic or narrative ones. The images and media with which we interact are selected for us based on their effectiveness in triggering specific neurological and psychological responses.

We are the kittens.

We are the kittens in the horizontal-striped boxes, whose neural patterns are played like notes on a guitar, shaping our perceptions, affects, behaviors, and worldviews. Some of us can only see vertical lines, others horizontal. We're gorging ourselves on mind-Doritos specifically designed to modulate our individual sensory and emotional responses. And just as Doritos are advanced psyops disguised as food, the images and texts we consume are sophisticated psyops disguised as information.

And it's about to get a whole lot weirder. But that's another conversation.

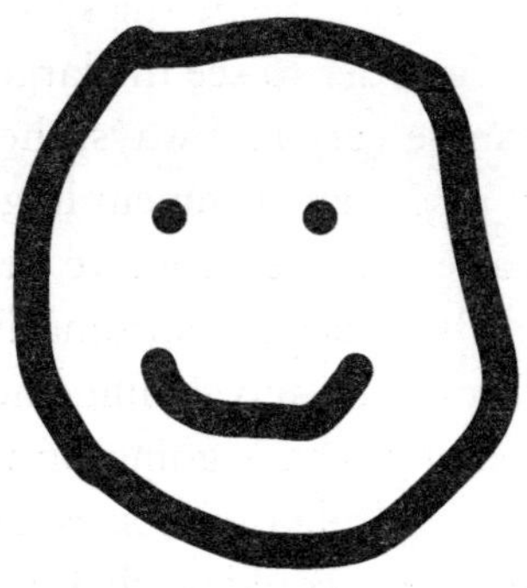

5

Society of the Psyop

We once looked at pictures. Then, with the advent of computer vision and machine learning, pictures started looking back at us. Now, something even stranger is happening.

Generative AI, adtech, recommendation algorithms, engagement economies, personalized search, and machine learning are inaugurating a new relationship between humans and media. Pictures are now looking at us looking at them, eliciting feedback and evolving. We've entered a protean, targeted visual culture that shows us what it believes we want to see, measures our reactions, then morphs itself to optimize for the reactions and actions it wants. New forms of media prod and persuade, modulate and manipulate, shaping worldviews and actions to induce us into believing what they want us to believe, and to extract value and exert influence.

What does it mean to live in a media environment that knows our wants, needs, vulnerabilities, emotional tics, kinks, and cognitive quirks far better than we do? That notices which kinds of stimulus induce what kinds of precognitive responses and uses machine learning to develop, A/B test, and deploy custom-generated cognitive injections designed to manipulate us even further, all without us consciously perceiving what's happening? And what does it mean to live in a media environments where this is all-pervasive: not only news and websites, videos and movies, but driving assistants in cars, AI-generated customer service representatives, search engines and chatbots, virtual HR managers, gas station pumps, smart houses and phones, and even washing machines … a media landscape

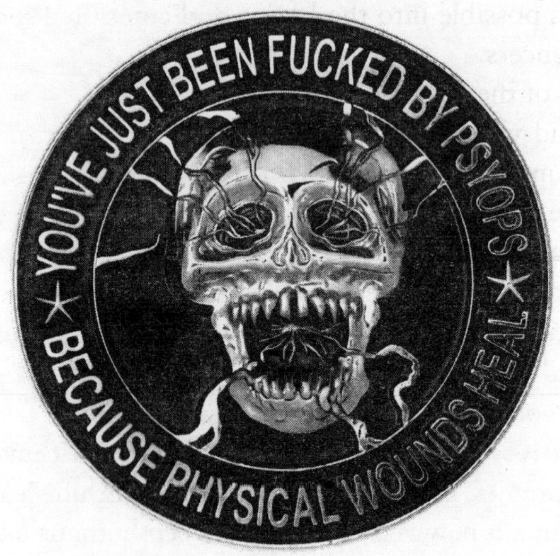

where your refrigerator, vibrator, and toothbrush collude with insurance companies, advertisers, political campaigns, and big retailers, using computer vision, machine learning, and biometric feedback to influence your behavior and worldview?

Every day, we are subject to subtle and not-so-subtle mind-control experiments. Through nearly imperceptible experiments and machine-learning-enabled analysis, coupled with various types of sensors (from simple "like" buttons and engagement metrics to cameras and other sensors designed to measure preconscious responses), the media we interact with seeks to develop a sense of—and make alterations to—each of our own unique neurological makeups.

If the postwar media landscape was characterized by spectacle, and the late twentieth and early twenty-first century by an age of surveillance, then we are entering a new phase. One marked by affective computing, machine-learning-enabled optimization, neuroscience, and cognitive psychology. A mediascape that has little use for distinctions between real and fake, signifier and signified. That assumes no distinction between perception and reality, even as it attempts to intervene as directly as possible into the brains and emotional makeup of its experiencers.

Society of the Psyop.[1]

How did we get here? This three-part essay traces a brief history of media, technologies, and techniques that take advantage of the malleability of perception, capitalizing on quirks in human brains to shape reality. It is a story about the manufacture of hallucinations and the fact that, under the right conditions, hallucination and reality can become one and the same.

Part 1

UFOs and the Future of Media

I first met Richard Doty in 2022. I was anxious. I could feel my unease rising as his silver SUV pulled into the parking lot across from the makeshift film studio where I was working at the University of New Mexico.[2] A paunchy man wearing a red polo shirt emerged. I wasn't afraid of physical violence. Rick Doty wasn't known for that. I was worried about my own sanity. Doty was known for that.[3]

Doty conducted elaborate psyop programs for the US Air Force in the 1970s and '80s. One of his targets, a defense contractor, was so consumed by paranoia after being subjected to Doty's craft that he was committed to a mental institution. There was also a well-respected journalist who, after enduring one of Doty's psychological operations, spent the remainder of her career babbling about reptoids, cover-ups, and ancient alien conspiracies. A third target, a former UFO investigator who collaborated with Doty, publicly confessed to participating in a military disinformation campaign and retreated into self-imposed obscurity. We would be spending the next two days together. It turned out that I liked the guy.

I had sought out Doty because I wanted to learn about the particular form of media-making he practiced to such dramatic effect. My intuition was that Doty's career as a cultural producer could shed some light on what media might be like in an age of recommendation algorithms, personalized news feeds, information bubbles, and generative AI.

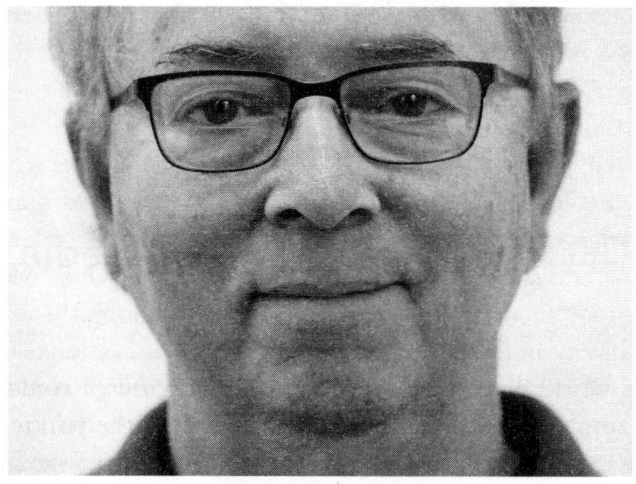

For the next two days, Doty explained the finer points of military interrogations and influence operations, the theory and practice of psyops, and how he'd created and used folklore about UFOs to develop counterespionage missions designed to protect classified Air Force assets. But in Doty's retelling of the work he did on behalf of the US military, there was a strange inversion. Yes, he created misinformation about UFOs to conceal the existence of secret US military projects. But he also described creating false stories about classified Air Force technologies to cover up the existence of actual UFOs (internally known as "cardinals," he claims). Upon retirement from the US Air Force, Doty became a self-styled whistleblower, recounting details of the real UFO program he claims to have had a hand in covering up. He told stories of a secret film documenting the existence of crashed saucers, a classified warehouse at Bolling Air Force Base containing the remnants of those UFOs, and the cultural life of captured pilots from the Zeta Reticuli star system.

Doty began working for the Air Force Office of Special Investigations in the late 1970s. AFOSI is an outfit analogous to an in-house FBI, charged with investigating criminal activity in the military and conducting counterintelligence work to ensure the security of military installations and assets. After completing his training in the Washington, DC, area, Doty was assigned to Kirtland Air Force Base in Albuquerque, New Mexico.

Kirtland is a massive complex, encompassing over 50,000 acres, extending from a collection of runways and hangars adjacent to the Albuquerque airport to vast tracts of land to the east and south. Its neighbors are a veritable who's who of conspiracy theories and UFO lore. Nestled among the mountains ninety miles to the north is Los Alamos National Labs, where World War II–era scientists worked in secret to develop the world's first atomic bomb. To the south is the Trinity site, where that atomic bomb was first detonated, turning the desert surface into a radioactive glass called "trinitite." Still further south is the White Sands Missile Range, where US forces transported Nazi rocket scientists in the aftermath of World War II as part of Operation Paperclip. The alleged Roswell UFO crash site is a two-hour drive southeast.

In the late 1970s, Kirtland Air Force Base's acknowledged tenants included the Air Force Weapons Laboratory, charged with research and development on advanced technology

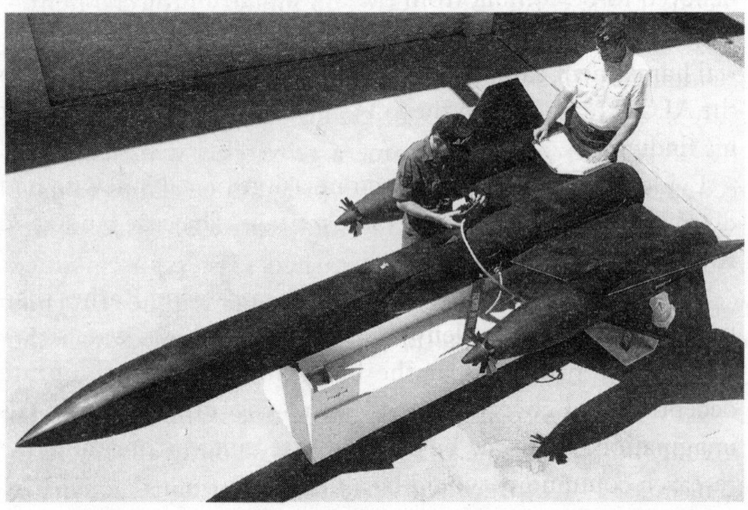

systems, directed-energy weapons, and the effects of nuclear fallout. Another outfit, Sandia National Labs, designed and tested components for nuclear weapons. Such weapons were stored and managed in a facility in a restricted section in the eastern part of the base. Kirtland also played host to a handful of unacknowledged tenants, including a detachment from the National Security Agency (NSA).

When Doty arrived in 1979, Kirtland was synonymous with top-secret military technology experiments. In 1973, base engineers had succeeded in using a ground-based laser to shoot down an airplane and were busy developing a directed-energy weapon that could be fired from an airborne platform. Elsewhere on the base, the Air Force trained Special Forces units, conducted advanced helicopter training, and tested experimental weapons systems. Doty's job was to keep all of this secret.

In the late 1970s, a military contractor named Paul Bennewitz, who lived on Kirtland's northern border, started seeing and photographing unusual lights and movements over the restricted range adjacent to his house. He came to the conclusion that they must be UFOs. An avid electronics enthusiast, Bennewitz made recordings of bizarre radio emissions he believed to be coming from the objects. Bennewitz offered to help the military repel what he believed to be an extraterritorial harassment campaign: He collected his evidence, sent it to the AFOSI team, and in the fall of 1980 was invited to present his findings.

Evidently, it was not an alien invasion that Bennewitz had discovered but a top-secret NSA program. The case landed on Rick Doty's desk.[4]

Doty took a creative approach to the problem: Rather than "neither confirm nor deny" the existence of UFOs or secret intelligence programs at the base, he staged an elaborate deception and cover-up operation to encourage Bennewitz's imagination. A source he'd recently recruited from the UFO research community would be a huge help.

In the summer of 1980, Doty made a pitch to this source, named William Moore, who was the coauthor (with Charles Berlitz) of the 1980 book *The Roswell Incident*. Doty's proposal was this: Doty would provide Moore with incontrovertible proof of extraterrestrial contact in exchange for Moore's help in conducting AFOSI investigations and reporting on the activities of amateur UFO groups. The deal was irresistible, and Moore cooperated.

Doty began using Moore as a proxy. Doty gave Moore doctored top-secret documents to pass along to Bennewitz, alluding to government knowledge of an extraterrestrial presence on earth. Furthermore, the documents implied that Bennewitz's discoveries were relevant to an above-top-secret program called "Aquarius," administered by a shadowy group called "MJ Twelve." An excerpt from the documents reads, in part:

> (S/WINTEL) USAF no longer publicly active in UFO research, however USAF still has interest in all UFO sightings over USAF installation/test ranges. Several other government agencies, led by NASA, actively investigates [*sic*] legitimate sightings through covert cover. (S/WINTEL/FSA) One such cover is UFO Reporting Center, US Coast and Geodetic Survey, Rockville, MD 20852. NASA filters results of sightings to appropriate military departments with interest in that particular sighting. The official US Government Policy and results of Project Aquarius is still classified top secret with no dissemination outside official intelligence channels and with restricted access to 'MJ Twelve'. Case on Bennewitz is being monitored by NASA, INS, who request all future evidence be forwarded to them through AFOSI, IVOE.

The operation against Bennewitz snowballed: According to William Moore, in the summer of 1981, AFOSI arranged for Bennewitz to receive a computer he could use to decipher the "alien" signals. The doctored computer spat out long streams

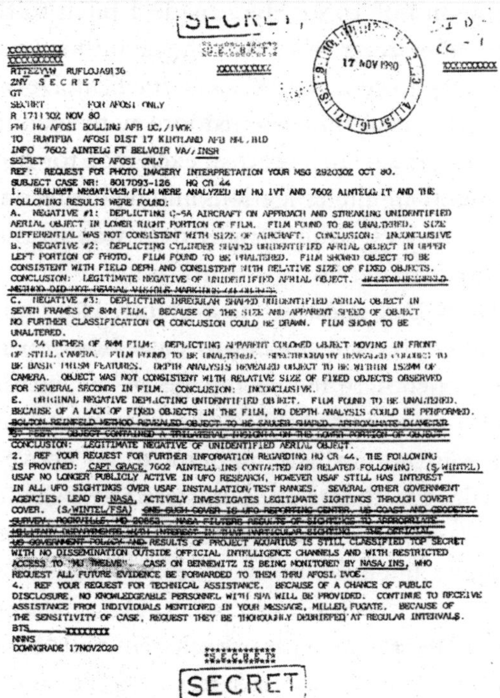

SECRET

17 NOV 1980

RTTEZYUW RUFLOJA9136
2NY S E C R E T
GT
SECRET FOR AFOSI ONLY
R 171130Z NOV 80
FM HQ AFOSI BOLLING AFB DC./IVOE
TO RUWIFBA AFOSI DIST 17 KIRTLAND AFB NM./BID
INFO 7602 AINTELG FT BELVOIR VA//INSR
SECRET FOR AFOSI ONLY
REF: REQUEST FOR PHOTO IMAGERY INTERPRETATION YOUR MSG 292030Z OCT 80.
SUBJECT CASE NR: 8017D93-126 HQ CR 44
1. SUBJECT NEGATIVES/FILM WERE ANALYZED BY HQ IVT AND 7602 AINTELG IT AND THE FOLLOWING RESULTS WERE FOUND:
A. NEGATIVE #1: DEPLICTING C-5A AIRCRAFT ON APPROACH AND STREAKING UNIDENTIFIED AERIAL OBJECT IN LOWER RIGHT PORTION OF FILM. FILM FOUND TO BE UNALTERED. SIZE DIFFERENTIAL WAS NOT CONSISTENT WITH SIZE OF AIRCRAFT. CONCLUSION: INCONCLUSIVE
B. NEGATIVE #2: DEPLICTING CYLINDER SHAPED UNIDENTIFIED AERIAL OBJECT IN UPPER LEFT PORTION OF PHOTO. FILM FOUND TO BE UNALTERED. FILM SHOWED OBJECT TO BE CONSISTENT WITH FIELD DEPH AND CONSISTENT WITH RELATIVE SIZE OF FIXED OBJECTS. CONCLUSION: LEGITIMATE NEGATIVE OF UNIDENTIFIED AERIAL OBJECT. [illegible]
C. NEGATIVE #3: DEPLICTING IRREGULAR SHAPED UNIDENTIFIED AERIAL OBJECT IN SEVEN FRAMES OF 8MM FILM. BECAUSE OF THE SIZE AND APPARENT SPEED OF OBJECT NO FURTHER CLASSIFICATION OR CONCLUSION COULD BE DRAWN. FILM SHOWN TO BE UNALTERED.
D. 34 INCHES OF 8MM FILM: DEPLICTING APPARENT COLORED OBJECT MOVING IN FRONT OF STILL CAMERA. FILM FOUND TO BE UNALTERED. SPECTROGRAPHY REVEALED COLORS TO BE BASIC PRISM FEATURES. DEPTH ANALYSIS REVEALED OBJECT TO BE WITHIN 152MM OF CAMERA. OBJECT WAS NOT CONSISTENT WITH RELATIVE SIZE OF FIXED OBJECTS OBSERVED FOR SEVERAL SECONDS IN FILM. CONCLUSION: INCONCLUSIVE.
E. ORIGINAL NEGATIVE DEPLICTING UNIDENTIFIED OBJECT. FILM FOUND TO BE UNALTERED. BECAUSE OF A LACK OF FIXED OBJECTS IN THE FILM, NO DEPTH ANALYSIS COULD BE PERFORMED. [illegible] CONCLUSION: LEGITIMATE NEGATIVE OF UNIDENTIFIED AERIAL OBJECT.
2. REF YOUR REQUEST FOR FURTHER INFORMATION REGARDING HQ CR 44, THE FOLLOWING IS PROVIDED: CAPT GRACE, 7602 AINTELG, INS CONTACTED AND RELATED FOLLOWING: (S/WINTEL) USAF NO LONGER PUBLICLY ACTIVE IN UFO RESEARCH, HOWEVER USAF STILL HAS INTEREST IN ALL UFO SIGHTINGS OVER USAF INSTALLATION/TEST RANGES. SEVERAL OTHER GOVERNMENT AGENCIES, LEAD BY NASA, ACTIVELY INVESTIGATES LEGITIMATE SIGHTINGS THROUGH COVERT COVER. (S/WINTEL/FSA) [illegible] RESULTS OF PROJECT AQUARIUS IS STILL CLASSIFIED TOP SECRET WITH NO DISSEMINATION OUTSIDE OFFICIAL INTELLIGENCE CHANNELS AND WITH RESTRICTED ACCESS TO "MJ TWELVE". CASE ON BENNEWITZ IS BEING MONITORED BY NASA/INS, WHO REQUEST ALL FUTURE EVIDENCE BE FORWARDED TO THEM THRU AFOSI, IVOE.
4. REF YOUR REQUEST FOR TECHNICAL ASSISTANCE. BECAUSE OF A CHANCE OF PUBLIC DISCLOSURE, NO KNOWLEDGEABLE PERSONNEL WITH SPA WILL BE PROVIDED. CONTINUE TO RECEIVE ASSISTANCE FROM INDIVIDUALS MENTIONED IN YOUR MESSAGE, MILLER, FUGATE. BECAUSE OF THE SENSITIVITY OF CASE, REQUEST THEY BE THOROUGHLY DEBRIEFED AT REGULAR INTERVALS.
BT
NNNS
DOWNGRADE 17NOV2020

SECRET

of quasi-nonsensical text as if it were a chatbot in a trance or fugue state:

> WE CANNOT TELL MILITARY OF THE US MAKING HUMANOIDS REASON FOR HATE IS YOU ARE GOOD—WE TRUST YOU TAKE VAST PORTION UNIVERSE AGAINST OUR AGGRESSION THE NUMBER OF OUR CRASHED SAUCERS IS EIGHT NERVE YOU WE REALIZE TELL THE TRUTH

Then the operation against Bennewitz became more elaborate. Knowing that Bennewitz was an avid amateur pilot and that he suspected the existence of a top-secret alien captive near the town of Dulce, New Mexico, AFOSI installed surplus military equipment on the top of Archuleta Mesa so that Bennewitz would see it on one of his flyovers and be convinced of the existence of the secret base. The Air Force was crafting an alternate reality to feed Bennewitz's predilections and ensure that he believed what they wanted him to believe.

With the Bennewitz project underway, Doty began a second operation involving Linda Moulton Howe, an award-winning television journalist who'd recently completed *A Strange Harvest*, a documentary on the "cattle mutilation" phenomena. In the wake of that success, Howe received a contract from HBO to make a second documentary on the topic of UFOs. Doty got in touch with Howe and invited her to Kirtland Air Force Base for a briefing. At the AFOSI offices, Doty explained that Howe was onto something big and that AFOSI was prepared to help. He then pulled out a dossier and instructed Howe that its contents were for her eyes only: She could read the documents but take no pictures. Other AFOSI officers observed her reaction from behind a one-way mirror.

Doty presented Howe with a dossier entitled "Briefing Paper for the President of the United States." The documents therein told a remarkable story of an ongoing extraterrestrial presence on Earth, UFO crashes at Roswell and other locations, and a surviving alien being held at Los Alamos. Moreover, the US government had reason to believe that aliens had genetically intervened in the human race and guided our development using various techniques, such as the creation of a great spiritual leader approximately two thousand years ago. Echoing the documents fed to Bennewitz, the dossier reiterated that the "MJ Twelve" group was responsible for the UFO and extraterrestrial program.

Doty explained to Howe that this was only the beginning. In return for Howe's coordination with AFOSI on her documentary, he promised footage from a top-secret film documenting an apocryphal 1964 UFO landing at Holloman Air Force Base in southern New Mexico and offered her access to an Air Force colonel who had allegedly handled one of the surviving aliens from the Roswell crash. Howe was thrilled. Weeks passed. Then months. No footage arrived; no interviews materialized. HBO killed the project. Howe's documentary on the UFO phenomenon was not going to happen.

The 1988 edition of the *US Army Field Manual* outlines ten principles of military deception. The "Monkey's Paw" principle states that the number of people with knowledge of a particular deception operation should be minimized, even if it means misleading one's own forces. "Jones's Dilemma" holds that deception becomes more difficult as the number of information channels available to the target increases, with the caveat that the greater number of *controlled* channels the target has access to, the more likely the deception will be successful. "Cry Wolf" holds that repeated mis-predictions of an event will desensitize the target to warnings of it. (This principle cites intelligence failures around the US Tet Offensive in Vietnam, which arose from repeated warnings that did not bear out.) Other principles involve the correct design and sequencing of misinformation, the importance of holding materials in reserve, and attention to the limits of human information processing.[5]

Doty's operation chiefly used a combination of three other principles: "Magruder's Principle—The Exploitation of Perceptions," the "Choice of Types of Deception" maxim, and "The Importance of Feedback." Both the field manual and Doty himself agree that the most important of these principles is "Magruder's Principle—The Exploitation of Perceptions." Named after the Confederate general John B. Magruder, it holds that "it is generally easier to induce the deception target to maintain a pre-existing belief than to deceive the deception target for the purpose of changing that belief." In this case, the preexisting belief that Doty capitalized upon was the existence of extraterrestrials and a government cover-up of that knowledge.

The "Choice of Types of Deception" maxim holds that the "deception planner should ... reduce the uncertainty in the mind of the target" and should "force him to seize upon a notional world view as being correct—*not making him less certain of the truth, but more certain of a particular falsehood*" (emphasis in original). To achieve this deception, Doty chose media tailored to each of his targets: For Bennewitz the engineer and pilot, he provided an advanced computer and a Potemkin base on a remote mesa; to Howe the journalist, he supplied false top-secret official documents and the promise of on-the-record sources with knowledge of the alien conspiracy.

Finally, the field manual emphasizes "The Importance of Feedback," the significance of which is "virtually self-evident." Feedback answers the question "Is anybody listening? (Is this channel effective?)" This is where William Moore, author of *The Roswell Incident*, came in. Moore was both a means of distribution and a feedback mechanism, a sensor that could judge the responses these particular media elicited. Doty could then gauge the reactions, amplify the signal that elicited the strongest feedback, and send back the amplified signal.

The outcome was a path to insanity. Paul Bennewitz became ever more paranoid about alien surveillance, accusing his wife of being controlled by aliens and eventually barricading himself in his house. In August 1988 he would be hospitalized for a

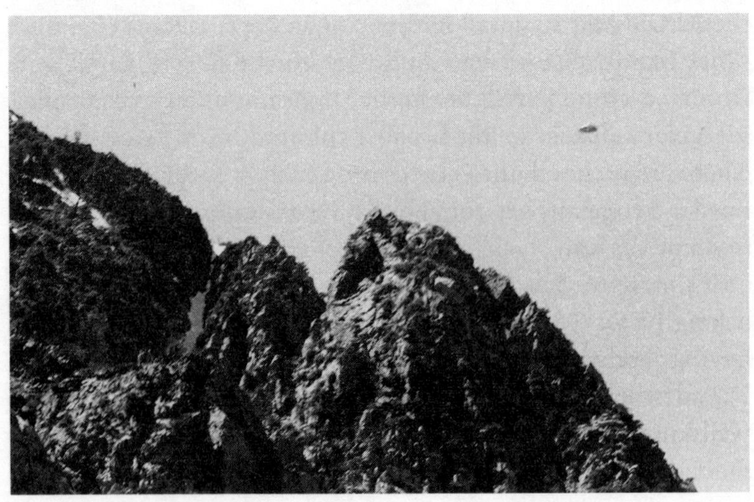

mental breakdown. The next summer, William Moore publicly confessed to participating in a disinformation campaign against Bennewitz and colluding with the US government to betray the UFO community. He faded into obscurity soon after. For her part, Linda Moulton Howe doubled down on her project to seek "the truth" about extraterrestrials. To this day, she claims that there are 168 advanced civilizations in the Milky Way, that multiple species of extraterrestrials inhabit Earth and can manipulate time, that there exists an alien presence under the ice sheets of Antarctica, that crop circles and cattle mutilations have something to do with it, and that a vast government conspiracy is covering it all up.

The information Doty fed to these three people gave life to what's known in UFO circles as the "darkside hypothesis." The story he told made its way through the UFO subculture and popped out into the mainstream as the plot of the television show *The X-Files*.

At this point, we might ask a simple question: Why? Was the top-secret NSA program at Kirtland so sensitive as to warrant the incredible resources spent to steer Paul Bennewitz into a reality populated by aliens? Did Linda Moulton Howe's reporting actually come close to something so important that the AFOSI had to derail her by producing a vast and detailed otherworldly conspiracy? And why bother recruiting William Moore, a prominent figure in the UFO community with only a marginal influence on the broader culture? And why use UFOs? There are no good answers to most of these questions, but we have a better answer for why UFOs became Doty's primary mimetic device.

It turns out that US military and intelligence agencies have a long history of using UFOs as a psychological instrument, having discovered their hyper-mimetic qualities in the 1950s. Decades before Doty's variations on the theme, UFOs were a well-known self-replicating cultural trope capable of infecting individual and cultural consciousness and spreading like a virus.

The discovery of the UFO hyper-meme took place in the 1950s, against the backdrop of a massive effort by US military and intelligence agencies to develop ways to manipulate people's minds. It was an era of CIA mind-control experiments, covert operations inspired by magic and illusionism, and extensive research into using computers, artificial intelligence, and electronic warfare to shape the experience of reality, and therefore reality itself.

Part 2

AI, Mind Control, and Magic

Brain warfare

It was the spring of 1953, and a lot of things were on the newly appointed CIA director Allen Dulles's mind. The plan to implement Operation Ajax, a coup to overthrow the democratically elected prime minister of Iran, Mohammad Mosaddegh, was in full swing and was only a few months away from implementation. A second plan, to overthrow the government of Guatemala, was under active development for the following year. But on April 10, something else was on the director's mind: "brain warfare."

> In the past few years we have become accustomed to hearing much about the battle for men's minds—the war of ideologies—and indeed our government has been driven by the international tension we call the "cold war" to take positive steps to recognize psychological warfare and to play an active role in it ... We might call it ... "brain warfare."[6]

Dulles was giving a speech to a group of Princeton alumni in Hot Springs, Virginia, that day. Standing before the crowd, Dulles described a psychological warfare program he believed to be taking place in Korea, China, and behind the Iron Curtain. "The brain under [Communist influence]," he remarked, "becomes a phonograph playing a disc put on its spindle by an outside genius over which it has no control." What on earth was he talking about?

A new form of media had appeared in American public life. In the midst of the Korean War, captured American prisoners made films confessing to the surreptitious use of biological and chemical weapons against Korean civilians. They wrote letters home extolling the virtues of their captors. Pilots and service members such as Floyd O'Neil, Paul R. Kniss, and Frank Schwable denounced the United States and confessed to war crimes. By the end of the war, more than half of all American POWs had signed statements denouncing the war and calling on the US to end the conflict. Some defected to North Korea.[7]

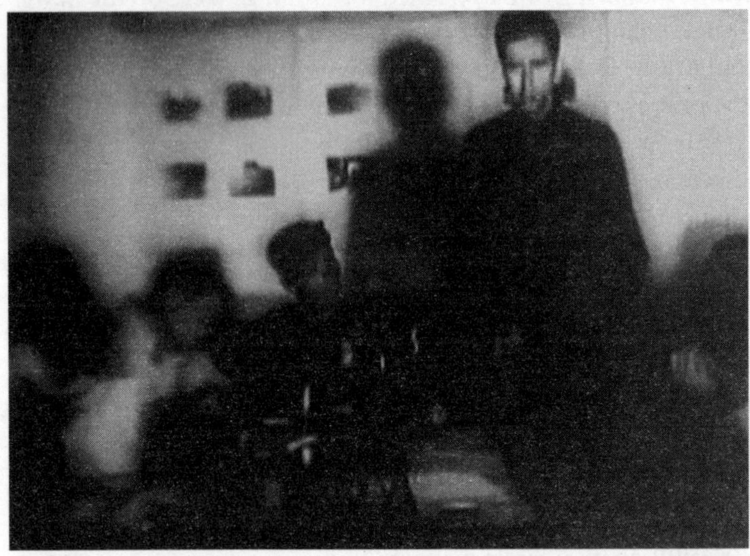

The CIA and US military were baffled. They were unable to imagine why American service members would participate in these propaganda efforts. Influenced by the work of Edward Hunter, an anti-communist journalist and CIA operative who popularized the term "brainwashing" in his sensational 1951 book *Brain-Washing in Red China: The Calculated Destruction of Men's Minds*, the government concluded that the Koreans (with Chinese backing) must be "brainwashing" their American captives.

If a "brainwashing" capability did exist, as the CIA believed, then there was a "brain warfare" gap. The Americans had no mind-control program. Three days after his speech in Hot Springs, Dulles authorized its creation.

Spearheaded by CIA chemist Sidney Gottlieb, MKUltra was a wide-ranging effort consisting of at least 149 subprojects investigating how the agency could use the human mind as a strategic and tactical arena of covert action, intelligence collection, and warfare. Over the next several decades, the CIA conducted and funded research into neuropsychology, mind control, brainwashing, LSD and other hallucinogenic drugs, hypnotism, sensory deprivation, artificial intelligence, radiation, and psychological torture. They conducted cruel experiments on unwitting students, soldiers, prisoners, drug users, sex workers, and the mentally ill.[8]

We have only scant documentation of MKUltra's scale and scope. On January 30, 1973, as journalists and congressional overseers started to learn about the program, CIA Director Richard Bissel dispatched Gottlieb to the agency's records center in Warrenton, Virginia, to destroy all documentation of the mind-control experiments.

What we know about the various MKUltra subprojects comes from a cache of nearly 20,000 documents, located during the 1977 Church Committee investigation, that survived Gottlieb's purge because they'd been stored at a different location.

From these surviving documents and other sources, we know that one area of research explicitly sought to use computers, early AI systems, and brain-computer interfaces to develop new forms of psychological warfare. Could the mind be programmed, erased, and reprogrammed like a computer or played like the "disc put on its spindle by an outside genius," as Dulles imagined? Could memories be implanted and deleted? Could humans' higher-order cognitive processes be circumnavigated to induce involuntary actions? Could the agency make a target hallucinate themselves into an alternate reality?

The answer would turn out to be "yes."

Face recognition and remote control animals

Woody Bledsoe was an early trailblazer in artificial intelligence, specializing in devising algorithms to conduct pattern matching, a crucial predecessor to modern machine learning. After receiving his PhD at UC Berkeley in 1953, he moved to New Mexico to work on nuclear weapons at Sandia Labs on the Kirtland Air Force Base complex. After a few years, Bledsoe went back to California and set up a research lab on the peninsula south of San Francisco in what would become modern Silicon Valley. He called the group Panoramic Research.

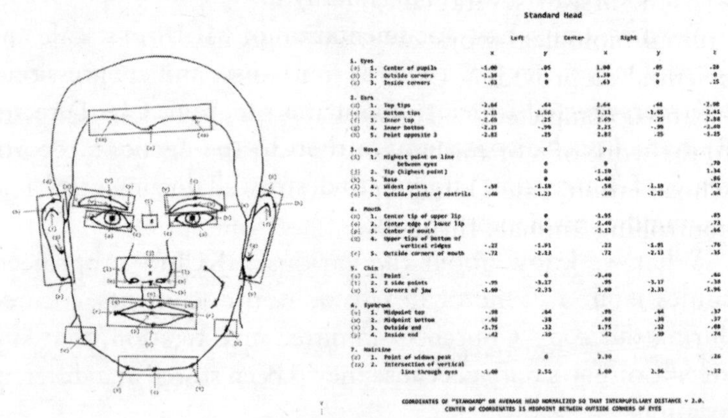

Standard Head

	Left x	Left y	Right x	Right y	z
1. Eyes					
(a) 1. Center of pupils	-1.00	.05	1.00	.05	.28
(b) 2. Outside corners	-1.38	0	1.38	0	0
(c) 3. Inside corners	-.63	0	.63	0	.25
2. Ears					
(d) 1. Top tips	-2.64	.44	2.64	.44	-2.98
(e) 2. Bottom tips	-2.11	-1.66	2.11	-1.65	-2.41
(f) 3. Inner top	-2.69	.25	2.69	.25	-2.88
(g) 4. Inner bottom	-2.21	-.90	2.21	-.90	-2.40
(h) 5. Point opposite 3	-2.82	.25	2.82	.25	-3.25
3. Nose		x	y		
(i) 1. Highest point on line between eyes		0	0		.70
(j) 2. Tip (highest point)		0	-1.10		1.34
(k) 3. Base		0	-1.40		.86
(l) 4. Widest points	-.58	-1.18	.58	-1.18	.47
(m) 5. Outside points of nostrils	-.40	-1.23	.40	-1.23	.94
4. Mouth					
(n) 1. Center tip of upper lip		0	-1.95		.85
(o) 2. Center edge of lower lip		0	-2.40		.73
(p) 3. Center of mouth		0	-2.12		.66
(q) 4. Upper tips of bottom of vertical ridges	-.22	-1.91	.22	-1.91	.76
(r) 5. Outside corners of mouth	-.72	-2.13	.72	-2.13	.35
5. Chin					
(s) 1. Point		0	-3.40		.46
(t) 2. 2 side points	-.95	-3.17	.95	-3.17	-.38
(u) 3. Corners of jaw	-1.90	-2.33	1.90	-2.33	-1.96
6. Eyebrow					
(v) 1. Midpoint top	-.98	.64	.98	.64	.37
(w) 2. Midpoint bottom	-.98	.38	.98	.38	.37
(x) 3. Outside end	-1.75	.32	1.75	.32	-.08
(y) 4. Inside end	-.42	.39	.42	.39	.74
7. Hairline					
(z) 1. Point of widows peak		0	2.30		.26
(zz) 2. Intersection of vertical line through eyes	-1.00	2.55	1.00	2.56	-.32

COORDINATES OF "STANDARD" OR AVERAGE HEAD NORMALIZED SO THAT INTERPUPILLARY DISTANCE = 2.0. CENTER OF COORDINATES IS MIDPOINT BETWEEN OUTSIDE CORNERS OF EYES

In 1963, the CIA—using the cutout company "King-Hurley Research Group"—contracted Bledsoe to develop a system that would use computers to identify people by looking at pictures of their faces.

Bledsoe found inspiration in the work of Alphonse Bertillon, one of the founders of biometrics in the late nineteenth and early twentieth century. He began photographing his associates and analyzing their faces, assigning keypoints to various facial features (the centers of the pupils, the inside corners of the eyes, the outside corners of the eyes, etc.) and measuring the distances between them. By synthesizing these measurements, Bledsoe created a mathematical abstraction of a human head he called the "standard head."

Bledsoe's idea was to use a computer to analyze photos of people, calibrate the result against the standard head, look for a pattern corresponding to an image in the database, and identify a specific person's face. Today Bledsoe is known as the grandfather of facial recognition.[9]

It wasn't Bledsoe's first CIA contract. In May 1959, he had received MKUltra funding to carry out something called Subproject 94, which involved "investigations on the remote directional control of activities of selected species of animals including mammals and feathered vertebrates."[10]

In the first of several contracts, the agency explained that "initial biological work on techniques and brain locations essential to providing conditioning and control of animals has been completed."[11] The agency was most likely referring to the work of a Spanish neuroscientist named José Delgado, whose lab at Yale University had shown the feasibility of controlling animals through an electronic brain implant (a

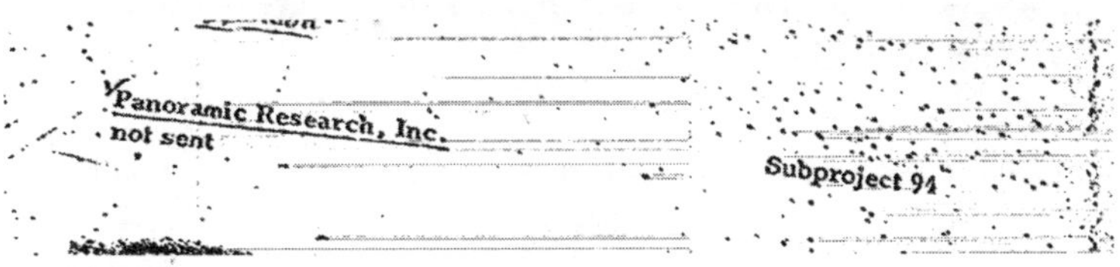

Panoramic Research, Inc.
not sent
Subproject 94

MEMORANDUM FOR: THE RECORD

SUBJECT : Project MKULTRA, Subproject No. 94

1. The purpose of this subproject is to provide a continuation of activities in selected species of animals. Miniaturized stimulating electrode implants in specific brain center areas will be utilized.

"stimoceiver") activated by remote control. In the 1950s and '60s, Delgado's experiments on animals and humans proved that a brain-computer interface could indeed be used to influence a subject's motor control, movements, and even emotions. Delgado reported that

> it is ... already possible to induce a large variety of responses, from motor effects to emotional reactions and intellectual manifestations, by direct electrical stimulation of the brain. Also, several investigators have learned to identify patterns of electrical activity (which a computer could also recognize) localized in specific areas of the brain and related to determined phenomena such as perception of smells or visual perception of edges and movements. We are advancing rapidly in the pattern recognition of electrical correlates of behavior and in the methodology for two-way radio communication between brain and computers.
>
> The individual is defenseless against direct manipulation of the brain because he is deprived of his most intimate mechanisms of biological reactivity. In experiments, electrical stimulation of appropriate intensity always prevailed over free will; and, for example, flexion of the hand evoked by stimulation of the motor cortex cannot be voluntarily avoided. Destruction of the frontal lobes produced changes in effectiveness which are beyond any personal control.[12]

It appears that Bledsoe's Subproject 94 was a covert version of Delgado's ongoing research at Yale, a shadow effort more easily adapted toward military or intelligence objectives than the public research conducted at the university.

Subproject 94 began in the summer of 1959 with experiments on rats and burros. By September, a CIA memo reported that "the feasibility of remote control of activities in two species of mammals has been demonstrated by limited trials" and that additional support for Bledsoe's project was required "in order to capitalize on this technical break-through." Bledsoe extended his experiments to dogs. In 1961, the agency reported that "performance is satisfactory" and it was proposed (it's unclear whether by Bledsoe or the CIA) that Subproject 94 begin "special investigations and evaluations ... toward the application of selected elements of these techniques to man."[13] Bledsoe was set to begin studying the effects of his methods on human beings.

But in 1962, something happened. The agency shut it all down. In November, the CIA wrote Bledsoe to inform him that the grant funding his research would not be renewed. In an internal memo, the CIA comptroller wrote that Subproject 94 had gone "off the rails," even as Sidney Gottlieb opined that "the overall performance [of Subproject 94] was highly satisfactory in all respects."[14]

The facial recognition contract came through shortly thereafter, keeping Panoramic Research solvent. But by 1966, Bledsoe was worn down from the constant hustle for funding and decided to go back to academia, taking a position as a professor of mathematics at the University of Texas at Austin. Panoramic Research ceased operations shortly thereafter.

We don't know whether Bledsoe's remote control mind experiments were ever tested on humans. The CIA burned their MKUltra records in 1973. Bledsoe burned much of his own archives in the 1990s after being diagnosed with amyotrophic lateral sclerosis (ALS) and realizing he would soon die.

It's not clear how well either of Bledsoe's CIA projects worked, but by the standards of the day, they impressed his agency overseers enough to warrant continued funding. With his facial recognition project, Bledsoe had set out on a path to use computers to "see" into the world of faces, and to potentially do things with those observations. With Subproject 94, he'd contributed to the development of a form of media that eschews images, representation, narrative, or abstraction and instead finds its purchase through the targeted insertion of instructions into a living brain, using direct neurological stimulation to elicit a desired emotion, behavior, or perception.

Computers "seeing" humans. Computers "controlling" humans. Operational media gone wild.

Across the country, another early experiment in artificial intelligence was taking place. This one, too, involved using computers and technology to capitalize on the quirks of our brains. It was an effort to create the illusion of a living computer.

ELIZA

At the Massachusetts Institute of Technology, Robert M. Fano, a protégé of Claude Shannon, founded and led the Project on Mathematics and Computation (Project MAC). With funding from the US Department of Defense's Advanced Research Projects Agency (ARPA), one of Project MAC's many endeavors involved inventing a system that allowed multiple researchers to network their computers together and share resources on a central mainframe. Computer networking was, of course, an important precursor to the contemporary internet.

If the networked MAC mainframe was an ur-form of the internet, then an odd program sitting on that mainframe was a ur-form of generative AI. It was an AI chatbot named ELIZA. Written by Joseph Weizenbaum, who would become one of history's most influential critics of artificial intelligence, ELIZA took the form of a digital therapist working in the style of Carl Rogers. Rogers's method emphasized "reflective listening," a form of active listening in which the therapist echoes the patient's statements back to them.

Users could interact with the program using natural language, a rarity at the time. The program worked by "asking" the user open-ended questions and using a simple algorithm to reflect the answers back:

User: Men are all alike
ELIZA: IN WHAT WAY
User: They're always bugging us about something or other
ELIZA: CAN YOU THINK OF A SPECIFIC EXAMPLE?
User: Well, my boyfriend made me come here
ELIZA: YOUR BOYFRIEND MADE YOU COME HERE
User: He says I'm depressed much of the time
ELIZA: I AM SORRY TO HEAR THAT YOU ARE DEPRESSED

Weizenbaum described his early work with computers, only somewhat ironically, as that of a "confidence man." In 1958, he'd written a simple program to play a game called Five in a Row, and the program could consistently beat any first-time player. He titled a paper describing the game "How to Make a Computer *Appear* Intelligent." The idea, he explained, "was to create the powerful illusion that the computer was intelligent," even as he described exactly how the program worked.[15]

ELIZA built on the illusion Weizenbaum first developed with Five in a Row. An apocryphal story holds that Weizenbaum's secretary spent hours "talking" to the chatbot and even asked Weizenbaum to "leave the room so that [she] and ELIZA could have a real conversation." As the circle of ELIZA's users spread, some began attributing consciousness to the script. Weizenbaum had succeeded in creating a powerful device for the manufacture of hallucinations.

The AI researcher was taken aback by the success of his conjuring: "I had not realized," Weizenbaum would write, "that extremely short exposures to a relatively simple computer program could induce powerful delusional thinking in quite normal people."[16]

Weizenbaum decided to dispel the illusion he'd created. He would do this by publishing ELIZA's source code. If he explained exactly how the trick worked, he surmised, he could dispel the "delusional thinking" the program prompted. "In the realm of AI ... machines are made to behave in wondrous ways, often sufficient to dazzle even the most experienced observer. But once a particular program is unmasked ... its magic crumbles away."[17]

But things didn't quite work out that way. He was horrified to learn that some users continued to believe that ELIZA was sentient, even after he revealed exactly how the magic trick worked. He was similarly horrified to learn that a colleague, Kenneth Colby, who wrote an analogous program called DOCTOR, sought to commercialize it as an ersatz therapist for mental health patients. Weizenbaum believed this to be highly unethical.[18]

With this simple script, Weizenbaum demonstrated something about the relationship between language, meaning, perception, and consciousness. ELIZA showed that when you create a string of words, the person who receives those words will attribute meaning to them, even if no meaning was intended (a process akin to refrigerator-magnet poetry or forms of experimental writing). In short, language doesn't require a speaker or writer's intention to "work."

In the context of ELIZA, this revealed a secondary magic trick. Because the user could derive meaning from the statements ELIZA made, the user would preconsciously attribute intentions to the program making the words. The user concluded that because the computer made some words and because those words were meaningful to the user, the computer must have intended to communicate those meanings. Thus, the computer was "intelligent."

With ELIZA, Weizenbaum realized that by using a set of reasonably simple linguistic and algorithmic tricks, the computer could create the illusion of an intelligent agent behind the words, a kind of "synthetic intentionality."[19] In the context of artificial intelligence, this act of conjuring became known as the "ELIZA effect."

The effect was similar to the explicit and implicit arguments

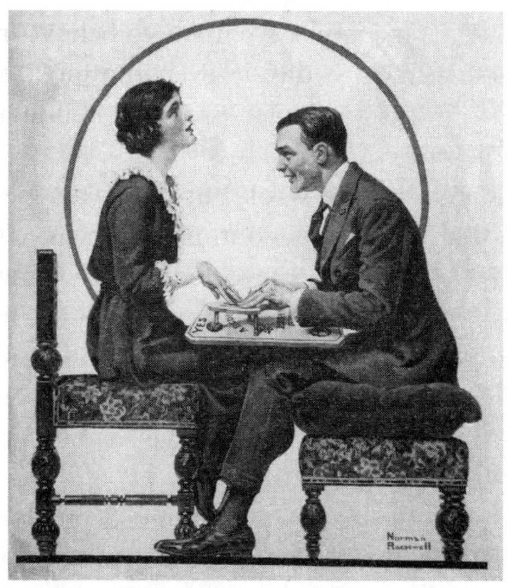

we find in other arenas: Religious fundamentalists argue that some things in the universe (e.g., humans, other life-forms, and, strangely, bananas) exhibit patterns we cannot imagine appearing through natural processes.[20] Therefore, those patterns must have a "creator" lurking behind them, ergo evolution is false and creationism is correct. A similar trick is at work in toys like the "Magic 8 Ball" or Ouija boards. Because the toys give sensible (albeit vague) answers to questions, they create the illusion that some supernatural intentionality must be lurking in the background, using the toy as a medium. That isn't to say that these forms of "synthetic intentionality" are always illusions: If you see writing in the sand on a beach, you assume someone wrote it with a stick. If you see elaborate crop circles in a cornfield …

Illusions or supernatural-seeming phenomena, whether chatbots, Ouija boards, or bananas, are prompts for the imagination. The prompt works by creating subtle cognitive contradictions. The preconscious part of perception intuitively ascribes intentionality, while the rational part of the brain wants to explain it away (which is sometimes impossible).

Which part of the brain "wins" in this situation? You must either "choose" to believe that something supernatural is truly happening, or you must find a way to rationalize or explain away a supernatural cause. Or, further, you can leave the source of the supernatural phenomena open-ended and unresolved, which is the most challenging. Preexisting beliefs play a strong role in this unconscious "choice" (magicians absolutely know this and use it to their advantage). We therefore find ourselves on fertile ground for the "Magruder Principle," as we saw in part 1, where a skilled practitioner doesn't waste effort trying to change an existing belief but, rather, scans for opportunities to amplify one that's already present.

Weizenbaum had discovered something at the core of the magician's art: the understanding that our perceptual experience has primacy over our logical faculties. We do not "see" and "hear" with our eyes and ears but with our preconscious minds; our ability to reason does not affect what we directly perceive. A skilled magician has a sophisticated understanding of how to exploit preconscious perceptions and the gap separating them from reason. They insert themselves into that space to bend our experience of reality.

Weizenbaum did not work for the CIA and was not intentionally engaged in work on psyops, but the type of conjuring he'd performed, and the subtle dynamics between perception and reality that he'd demonstrated, were of great interest to the agency. The CIA was absolutely interested in magic—so much so that one of the very first people they brought into MKUltra was a magician.

Magic

We can think of magic as a type of media—one that operates in the world of preconscious perception, playing with associations, expectations, symbols, and other forms of media to alter experience, to influence behavior, to affect the physical world, and to produce any number of other effects. To study magic is to study the quirks, foibles, and everyday hallucinations that characterize human perception, and to use those gaps between reality-as-it-is and reality-as-it-is-perceived as a vehicle for making supernatural-seeming interventions into perceived reality.[21]

As a form of media, magic operates in a perceptual landscape of associations and forces that have little to do with reason or logical perception. Lionel Snell (aka Ramsey Dukes), an early progenitor of "chaos" and "postmodern" magic, observes that

> our brains have evolved a non-logical data processing facility which is, in its own way, every bit as useful and sophisticated as reason but which we tend to play down or analyze away because its causal connections seem so tenuous. This facility, which I called "feeling," acts much faster than reason and seems to process vast amounts of data in parallel rather than sequentially like a logical thought.[22]

Snell explains that what we call "feeling" or "intuition" is the result of our having unconsciously internalized and classified huge amounts of perpetual "patterns" with varying levels of abstraction and complexity. For example, we may have preconsciously learned that walking alone at night and seeing a group of loud drunken men in the distance "goes with" danger, that green meat "goes with" feelings of sickness, or that shuffling a deck of cards "goes with" randomness.

In theoretical literature on magic, there are numerous schools of thought about what magic "is," and each understands the gap between perception and reality in different ways. For our purposes, we will make a vastly oversimplified distinction between "stage magic" and "magick." The theory underlying stage magic holds that reality is relatively stable but our perceptions of it are glitchy. By capitalizing on the eccentricities of preconscious perception, we can create illusions, feats of wonder, or supernatural-seeming outcomes. In stage magic, supernatural-seeming feats are all "false." The art of magic is therefore the art of deception, of creating phenomena that are not real but that appear to be so. As James "the Amazing" Randi put it: "Magicians are the most honest people in the world: They tell you they're going to fool you, and then they do it."

In contrast, theories of "magick" are not so confident about distinctions between true and false or illusion and reality. There is a much bolder claim: Perception and reality cannot be disentangled, and so they actually are, for practical purposes, one and the same.[23] Because we cannot know "reality" beyond our perceptions, we can make no functional distinction between the two. In practice, the craft of magick suggests that by altering our perceptions, we can effectively alter reality itself.[24]

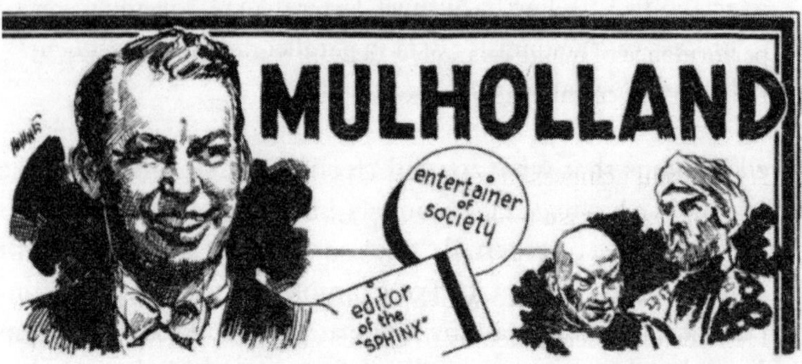

The CIA's staff magician was neither a spiritualist nor a postmodernist. John Mulholland (born John Wickizer) was a master illusionist, public intellectual, and stage magician. Born in Chicago in 1896, Mulholland's fascination with magic began at the age of five when his mother took him to see a performance by the legendary Harry Kellar. A few years later, they relocated to New York City, where Mulholland quickly immersed himself in the magic community. He joined the Society of American Magicians and convinced Kellar and John William Sargent to take him under their wing, becoming a professional stage magician while still a teenager. Over the next few decades, Mulholland ascended to become one of the premier performers of his day and authored more than a dozen books on magic, illusionism, its history, and its relevance to communication and psychology. From 1930, he served as the editor for *The Sphinx*, a trade journal for magicians, alongside his wife Pauline Pierce and their polyamorous partner Dorothy Wolf, his longtime assistant.

For Mulholland, magic had little to do with the supernatural. He was highly skeptical of claims about the paranormal. Far from involving some kind of otherworldly conjuring, for Mulholland, magic

> is the pretended performance of those things which cannot be done. The success of a magician's simulation of doing the impossible depends upon misleading the minds of his audiences ... A performance of magic is largely a demonstration of the universal reliability of certain facts of psychology.[25]

> A magician achieves his effects not because the hand is quicker than the eye—it isn't—but because the eye is easily tricked into seeing what it expects to see, what the mind tells it to see.
>
> Magic is a maze into which the magician lures his audience. He adds extraneous details to clutter and confuse their minds. Then he leads them, by misdirection, to take the wrong turn. For it is not only our eyes that play tricks on us. Memory, too, leads us astray.[26]

One of Mulholland's professional hobbies was using his knowledge of trickery and deception to question the claims of psychics, mediums, and charlatans purporting to have access to the supernatural. His 1938 book *Beware Familiar Spirits* set out to refute the extravagant claims of spiritualists and mediums. In 1952, he wrote an article for *Popular Mechanics* debunking the UFO phenomenon.

In early 1953, Mulholland disappeared from public life. He closed up shop at *The Sphinx* and canceled most of his professional commitments. On the record, Mulholland had concerns about his health. In reality, the magician had accepted a position in the CIA's newly formed MKUltra program.[27] (The security-clearance process had gone slowly due to the agency's nervousness about Mulholland's "sexual proclivities.") As he transitioned from public figure to clandestine operative, his income from performing and publishing was replaced by a stream of checks from an obscure organization with a mailbox at Southern Station, Washington, DC, named "Chemrophyl Associates."[28]

Like other stage magicians, Mulholland's oeuvre was built upon the premise that our minds make sense of the world around us through a constant process of preconscious pattern matching. When our minds encounter a familiar pattern such as a person tying their shoelaces or the appearance of a coin in our hand, our minds tend to preconsciously "throw away" those observations for having no particular relevance. The art of magic involves, in part, mimicking patterns that produce those "throwaway" observations or perceptual blind spots, and using them as a wrapper for an unexpected payload—a rabbit coming out of a hat, for instance. When the payload is revealed, it appears to have a supernatural origin because our minds have preconsciously "thrown away" the wrapper that contained it.

A payload might be delivered using a pattern rendered imperceptible by materials to which nonspecialists lack a strong memetic relationship. Most people rarely think about invisible thread, for instance, so a magician can capitalize on an audience's lack of experience with that material to produce the illusion of something to which we have a far stronger memetic relationship: levitation, for example. For the nonspecialist, the memetic content of watching an object levitate is far more salient than what a fellow magician might perceive, namely, a magician using invisible thread to create the appearance of a levitating object.

There are, of course, numerous other ways to deliver a "magical" payload (misdirection, concealment, forcing, etc.), but in Mulholland's paradigm, all exploit the simple fact that our minds either throw away, selectively interpret, or even act upon the vast majority of our sensory stimulus based on our preconscious and/or memetic priors. In other words, for Mulholland the art of magic has little to do with the supernatural. Instead, magic is the art of the cognitive-injection attack, or mind hacking.

Mulholland had several projects for the CIA. Subproject 4 was an assignment to write a top-secret manual entitled *The Art of Deception*, instructing CIA field officers on using the fundamentals of magic to conduct more effective covert operations. Mulholland's manual, eventually published in 2009 as *The Official CIA Manual of Trickery and Deception*, contained recipes for covert communications, the surreptitious delivery of toxins, hiding sensitive data and people, altering one's appearance and mannerisms, and capitalizing on the different social expectations of men and women.

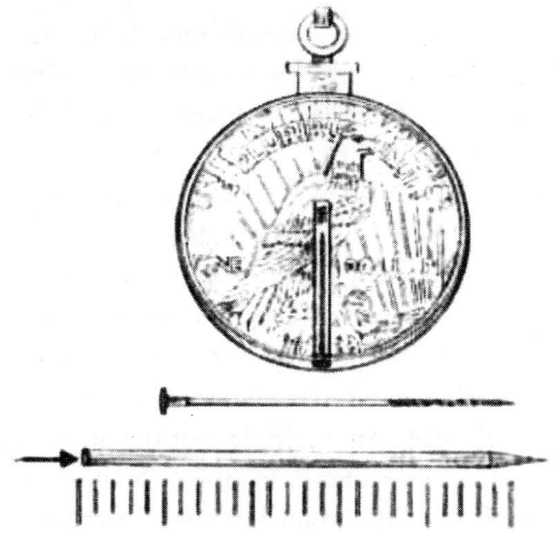

The methods he devised often relied on concealing something remarkable inside something ordinary. He devised a stealthy communication technique that involved tying shoelaces in various ways to communicate messages, useful in communicating something by simply walking past someone on the street. He designed a version of the "disappearing box" (which makes the person who enters it "disappear") into the trunk of a car, useful in the exfiltration of CIA agents from hostile situations. Another of his inventions was a silver dollar coin modified to contain a hidden needle to deliver deadly poison.

Like computer viruses masquerading as run-of-the-mill software updates, Mulholland's inventions transformed the world of everyday objects and gestures into an invisible means of manipulation and covert action. The ordinariness of his inventions was precisely what made them effective.

Magick

An electronic signal sent directly into the brain of a hapless dog. The words of an early chatbot conjuring a spectral, techo-supernatural intelligence. An innocent-looking coin containing a powerful poison spike.

Bledsoe, Weizenbaum, and Mulholland were developing and refining an odd assortment of media, united by their ability to bypass reason and the sensible, to speak directly to the mind's nether regions and to elicit precognitive responses. Media designed to fly below the radar of rationality to shape experiences, beliefs, and consciousness in ways that dissolve boundaries between perception and reality, the material and the immaterial, and the natural and the supernatural.

Woody Bledsoe, Joseph Weizenbaum, John Mulholland, and various branches of the CIA developed and deployed media designed to inject alternate realities into their subjects' minds. Yet they all understood themselves to be in the business of artifice, of creating things that were not "real." Weizenbaum joked that he was a "con man," while Mulholland always maintained that magic involved "misleading the minds of his audience." They were creating things that did not exist in order to cover up things that did exist, or to manipulate their targets into believing, and therefore acting, in ways they wanted to take advantage of.

Nonetheless, in their larger worldviews, these were mere magic tricks. Rabbits coming out of hats were actually coming out of specially designed tables. Tricks are meant to deceive and distort, to be sure, but they can have no bearing on reality itself, whose metaphysical foundations remained immune from such illusionistic knob twisting.

But what if they were wrong?

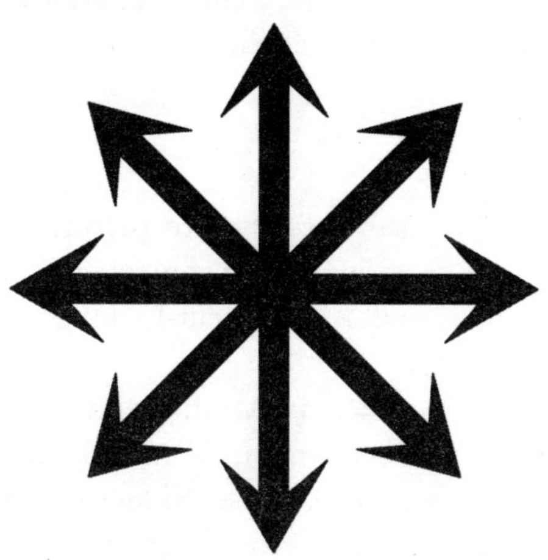

What if they believed they were practicing stage magic but were in fact playing with something far more occult? What if they were inadvertently playing with magick?

And what would happen if their sleights of hand, electronic signals, and sigils began conjuring different types of rabbits? Magickal beings with their own ideas about the malleability of perception and reality?

Mulholland's experience debunking the supernatural made him useful to the agency. The CIA had become fascinated by the possibilities of hypnosis, extrasensory perception, telepathy, and other parapsychological phenomena. Mulholland became their internal reality check. By 1955, Mulholland was traveling around the country to meet and assess psychic test subjects engaged in an early version of "remote viewing," a man who claimed that a copper-lined Faraday cage gave him enormous psychic abilities, and other *X-Files*-inflected occurrences.

In 1956, the CIA gave Mulholland another task: investigating UFOs.

UFOs had taken to the skies. And the CIA knew all about them—because the CIA had created them.

Part 3

Cognition and Chaos

October 1962, Havana Bay, Cuba

Global thermonuclear war was imminent. Soviet nuclear missile installations in Cuba were powered up and online. The situation had turned hot. Above the eastern part of the island, a Soviet surface-to-air missile streaked through the sky, tearing through an American U-2 spy plane and killing the pilot. Below, F-101 "Voodoo" fighters conducting low-level surveillance returned to base shredded by antiaircraft fire.

In Washington, President John F. Kennedy ordered the Strategic Air Command set to DEFCON 2, one step from nuclear war. SAC powered up a hundred intercontinental ballistic missiles and ordered twenty-three B-52s carrying nuclear weapons to fly circular patterns just out of Soviet airspace. Another fifteen hundred nuclear-armed bombers were put on high alert. More than a hundred and fifty F-106 "Delta Dart" interceptors—designed to fire and explode tactical nuclear missiles into fleets of incoming bombers—were put on fifteen-minute alert status.

The seas tightened. Four US Navy carrier groups formed a red line from the Bahamas to Puerto Rico, sealing off Cuba from the rest of the world. A Soviet cargo ship, the *Bucharest*, slipped through. Two more, the *Kimovsk* and the *Yuri Gagarin*, steamed in from the Atlantic in a game of chicken.

The CIA decided it was time for a UFO to make an appearance.

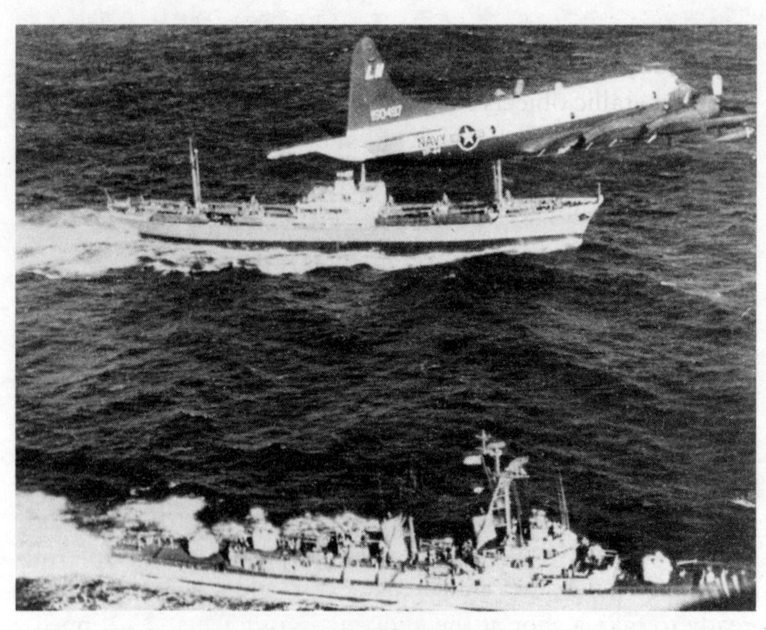
NAVY

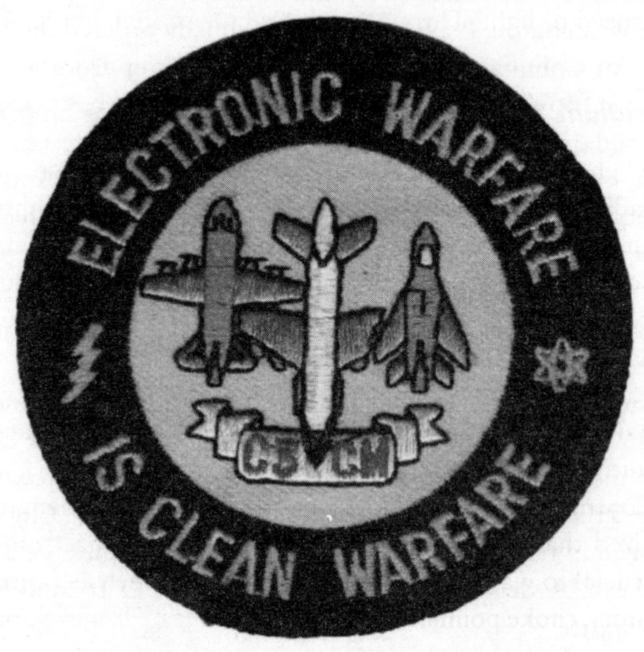
ELECTRONIC WARFARE
IS CLEAN WARFARE

An American submarine quietly slipped in close to Havana Bay, gently surfacing just long enough to let loose a handful of odd metallic objects suspended inside balloons. The devices slowly rose into the sky while the submarine slipped away. Just past the horizon line, a Naval destroyer hosting teams from the CIA and NSA activated a new top-secret electronic warfare system, code-named Palladium.

Cuban radar operators' sensor systems lit up, indicating an unidentified aircraft screaming toward Havana. NSA linguists and signals-intelligence technicians listened in as MiGs scrambled to intercept the unknown intruder. CIA controllers guided the UFO to stay just ahead of the fighters' line of sight, while sensors onboard the Palladium system ingested valuable information about the range, sensitivity, and electronic signatures of the Soviet detectors.

The Cuban fighter pilot reported weapons armed. He was ready to take a shot at the ghostly aircraft. The CIA flipped a switch. The UFO was gone. Blinked out of existence. Faster than the speed of light. Through an interdimensional wormhole.[29]

Palladium, or, How to make anything look like anything

The "ghost planes" (as the CIA called them) conjured by the Palladium system emerged from an insight into the changing nature of warfare. Command and control was once the domain of scouts, lookouts, signal corps, passenger pigeons, bugles, and smoke signals. The Second World War saw much of this replaced by technologies that used electromagnetic waves and electronics: sensors, sonar, radio, radar, and the like. The operational theater had transformed into a blend of the electronic, cognitive, and material.

Confronted with this new environment, military engineers realized that control over the electromagnetic spectrum was as crucial to war fighting as traditional aims such as capturing territory, choke points, and strategic facilities. The development of electronic command-and-control systems gave rise to technologies designed to thwart those systems: jamming devices, electronic countermeasures (ECM), and electronic counter-countermeasures (ECCM). Whoever could most effectively control the electromagnetic spectrum would have an advantage. Winston Churchill dubbed this contest "the battle of the beams." Technologies and techniques used in the electromagnetic battlespace became known as *electronic warfare*.

Throughout the Cold War, systems like Palladium began taking advantage of this new electro-optical landscape to synthesize electronic warfare with psyops.

In the 1950s, the CIA started to think about designing objects whose shapes, thermal signatures, and other forms of "appearance" could be tailored in particular ways whichever enemy systems would be doing the "looking." From then on, military technologies could and would be built with electronic warfare in mind.

Nearly a decade before the Cuban missile crisis, the CIA began collaborating with Lockheed's "Skunk Works" on a dramatic new approach to aerial surveillance. The U-2 was designed to reliably cruise at over 70,000 feet, an altitude much higher than any other military asset. The agency believed the U-2 to be invulnerable to interception and radar detection. By August 1955, the first prototype was undergoing flight tests above Groom Lake in Nevada.

When the plane began operational missions over the Soviet Union the following year, the agency got a surprise. Sensors onboard the U-2 revealed that adversarial systems could indeed track the plane. It was only a matter of time until the Soviets figured out how to shoot it down. That day came on May 1, 1960, when U-2 pilot Gary Powers was brought down over Sverdlovsk, creating an international incident. In his pocket was one of magician John Mulholland's inventions, a silver dollar containing a concealed poison spike. The coin could be used as a hidden weapon or as an undetectable means of

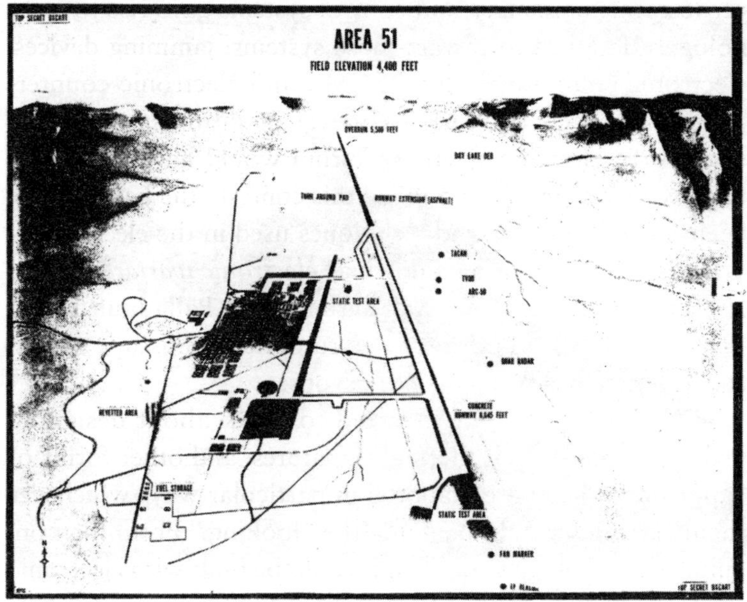

committing suicide. The Gary Powers incident ended U-2 overflights of the Soviet Union.

Long before Powers's capture, the CIA knew that the U-2's days were numbered. They had already begun work on an improved spy plane, codenamed Project OXCART. The new plane, which would become known as the A-12, would be the fastest air-breathing aircraft ever built. Like the U-2, it was built to outfly weapons systems, but it would do something else. The Gary Powers incident was a lesson in the physical vulnerability of machines. But there was a second lesson about the vulnerability of perception. Powers's U-2 had fallen prey to Soviet radar, but only because Soviet radar was able to "see" the plane. The U-2's successor would attempt to remedy that.

From the outset, OXCART was designed to be as invisible as possible to electronic sensors. To reduce the airplane's radar cross section, engineers designed the plane with curved surfaces, razor-sharp edges, inward-tilted rudders, and as much radar-absorbent coating as possible.

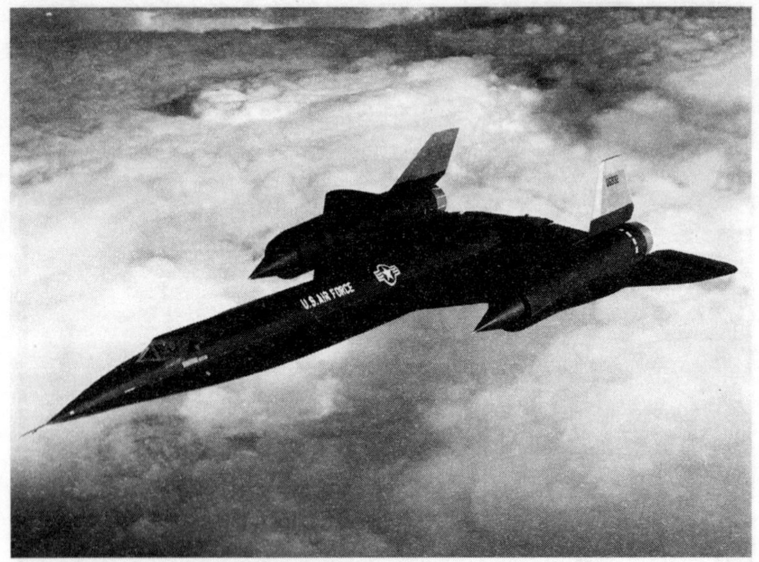

Along the way, OXCART engineers realized there was much more to "stealth" than simply making airplanes invisible to sensor systems. The principles behind stealth, combined with electronic countermeasures, could be used to make anything look like anything else, depending on which system was doing the looking.

The Palladium system was designed to create hallucinations. It worked by intercepting Soviet radar signals and then modifying them before returning the signal to the adversarial radar. The CIA could use this technique to make an enemy sensor system "see" whatever the agency wanted it to see. The idea was to create objects that looked completely different depending on who and what was doing the looking. Objects might, for example, look like a fleet of bombers to an early-warning radar, or a UFO if seen from a surface-to-air missile system. If fighters scrambled to find the object, they might see something like a metallic cube suspended inside a balloon. A pilot who encountered such an object might question their sanity and think twice about reporting it.

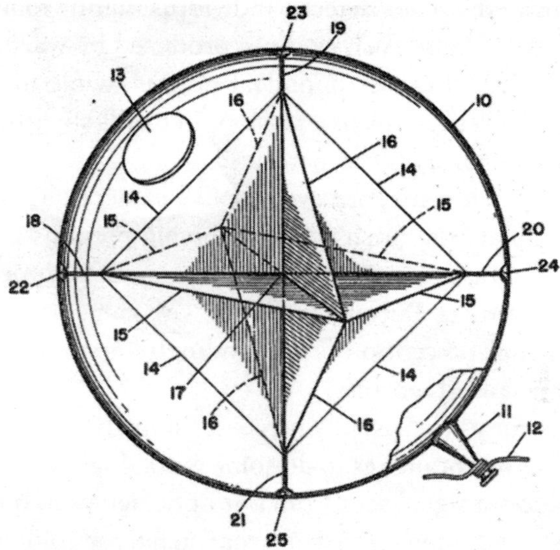

Palladium was an early example of hybrid technologies designed to weaponize the peculiarities of both electronic and human perception: to synthesize psyops with advanced technology to create weapons that attack adversaries' electronic sensors, equipment, and human minds.[30] Palladium was a precursor to what is now called "cognitive warfare," a philosophy of war making that takes advantage of the fact that the blend of the electronic, cognitive, and material that emerged in early military command-and-control systems has become the stuff of everyday life.

We are media

Every sensor system "sees" the world differently. An electro-optical satellite "sees" radiation reflected in visible wavelengths ("visible light"). A radar system emits a powerful electromagnetic signal using a specific frequency and looks for where that signal is reflected back to it. Sonar works similarly but uses acoustic signals because water absorbs and disperses radar waves. Infrared sensors detect bandwidths slightly longer than those of visible light, such as those produced by warm bodies or quickly retreating astronomical objects, while ultraviolet sensors detect reflections or emissions in bands slightly shorter than what human eyes can perceive.

In a very basic sense, our eyes are like cameras. They use an iris to modulate the intensity of incoming photons and have lenses to focus visible light onto an array of photoreceptor cells in our retinas. But the analogies with cameras end there. Human visual perception is astoundingly more complicated than any technical sensor.

In order for us to "visually perceive" something, rather than just "see" it, our brain has to do some work. Light entering our eyes produces a signal sent from our optic nerves to our visual cortex for processing, evaluating that signal for color, motion, and depth before we become consciously aware of what we're seeing. Depending on the intensity and complexity of that signal and the type of attention we give it, this process can take between 150 and 250 milliseconds on average.

It's incredibly slow. If we truly had a tenth to a quarter of second "lag time" between a visual perception and our reaction to it, we would be exceptionally clumsy. We wouldn't be able to accurately drive cars, shoot arrows, catch balls, or perform any number of everyday tasks. And yet we drive cars relatively safely, hit baseballs, and avoid obstacles while running. How are we able to do that given the sluggishness of our visual system?

It turns out that our mind has a "hack" for this. Our mind makes predictions about what it thinks we will see and shows us hallucinated projections of the near future. When a baseball batter sees a ball traveling toward them, they're not seeing the actual ball, but a hallucinated projection of where the mind thinks the ball will travel. The batter swings at the hallucination. If all goes well, the hallucinated ball is temporally synched to where the actual ball should be.

When we zoom out from the mechanics of motor function

and temporal synchronization, the story of visual perception becomes even more unstable. Our perceptions are not fixed or objective; they are profoundly relational, shaped by a network of influences: memories, expectations, cultural frameworks, and personal subjectivities.

Magicians have long understood how malleable perception truly is. They exploit it by "forcing" us to see what they want us to see, using subtle cues to guide our interpretation of events. The magician's "patter"—their seemingly casual dialogue with the audience—is far more important than most people realize. It's not just filler but a psychological primer. When a magician tells us that we are about to see someone levitate, they plant a seed in our minds. That seed grows into an interpretive framework through which we unconsciously process what happens next. We don't just see the trick; we see it through the lens the magician has given us. And so, when the levitation occurs, we don't question it. We literally see it, in part because our perception has been primed in advance to see it that way.[31]

"The relationship between the individual and the environment is so extensive that it almost overstates the distinction between the two to speak of a relationship at all," explains cultural neuroscientist Bruce Wexler.[32]

All of this has a profound implication. Media isn't something external to us that we passively receive and actively interpret but is a fundamentally constitutive part of us. In a very literal sense, we are media.

If perception and reality are so entwined that they cannot be meaningfully disentangled, then the world is far more "magickal" than common sense would seem to dictate.

Cognitive warfare / cognitive chaos

The MKUltra program never really went away. In the early days, it was animated by the theory of "brainwashing"—that you might be able to read and write the contents of a human

SECRET//SI//REL TO USA, FVEY

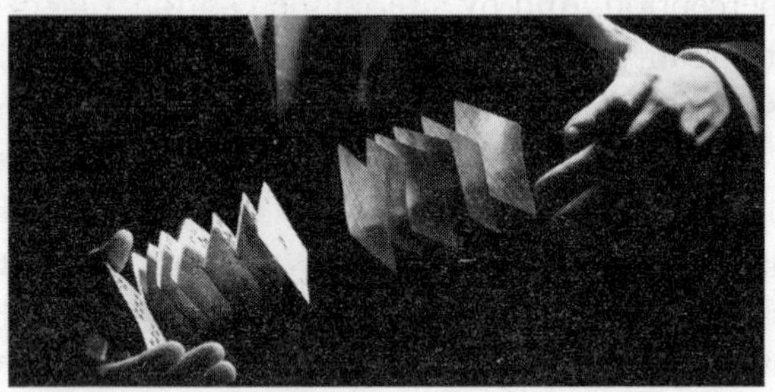

We want to build Cyber *Magicians.*

SECRET//SI//REL TO USA, FVEY

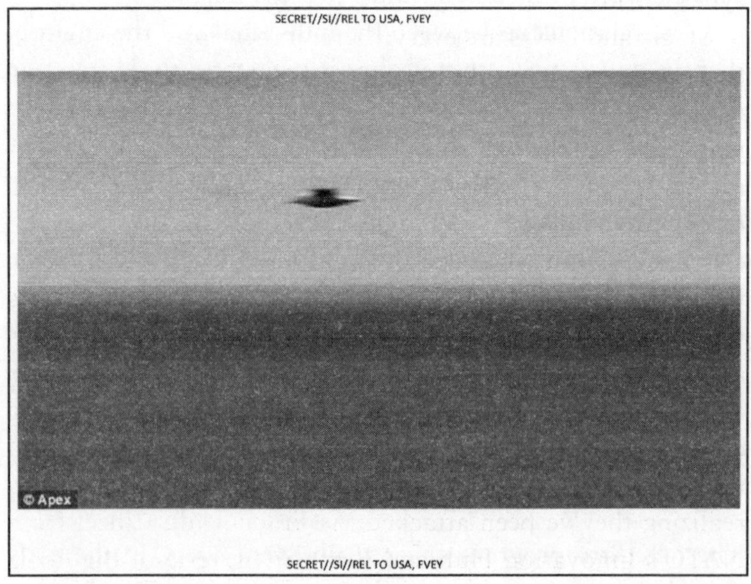

mind in ways analogous to data on a computer. Over time, this morphed into a different paradigm: Computers and networks could be used to take advantage of the cognitive quirks of human perception. And by altering perception, one can effectively alter reality.

This shift became clear in 2014, when the *Intercept* published a remarkable slide deck from the archive amassed by whistleblower Edward Snowden revealing the operations of the Joint Threat Research Intelligence Group, a unit of the British Government Communications Headquarters. JTRIG's playbook of "dirty tricks" includes an array of psychological operations that blur the lines between physical and cybernetic worlds: false flag operations, fake victim blog posts, disinformation campaigns, malware, "honey traps," and operations aimed at discrediting individuals and organizations. In short, the self-described goal of JTRIG operations is to use "online techniques to make something happen in the real or cyber world."

Magic and UFOs are everywhere in their internal presentation. Updating John Mulholland's MKUltra work for the age of the internet, JTRIG describes its goal as creating "cyber magicians." Elaborate charts show how to use principles of magic to conduct online covert actions and provide a menu of cognitive-injection techniques. And, of course, UFOs are everywhere in the slide deck.

"Cognitive warfare" is one of the buzzwords in today's military and intelligence literature, where the mind is described as warfare's "sixth domain" alongside land, sea, air, space, and cyber. Cognitive warfare goes beyond influencing opinion or spreading propaganda; its goal is to reshape reality itself through the minds of human targets, often without them even realizing they've been attacked. As François du Cluzel from NATO's Innovation Hub and Bernard Claverie of the Ecole Nationale Supérieure de Cognitique describe, cognitive warfare is "the art of using technology to alter the cognition of human targets, who are often unaware of any such attempt" to attack an adversary by "altering [their] representation of reality."[33]

Postscript

Once, we looked to military technology for glimpses of the future. Faster-than-a-bullet airplanes, global communication and targeting systems, space-based imaging platforms, and the like. Nowadays we find much of this technology in our personal electronic devices. And just as we carry around miniature commercialized spy satellites, GPS systems, and instant global telecommunications in our pockets, so do we also carry around miniature commercialized versions of the psyops of the past. There is, however, one enormous difference: Just as satellite imaging and GPS navigation has become inexpensive and ubiquitous, so have psyops.

Historically, targeted psyops, like targeted surveillance, were limited by the fact that they were very expensive. The covert magic devices crafted by John Mulholland for the CIA's

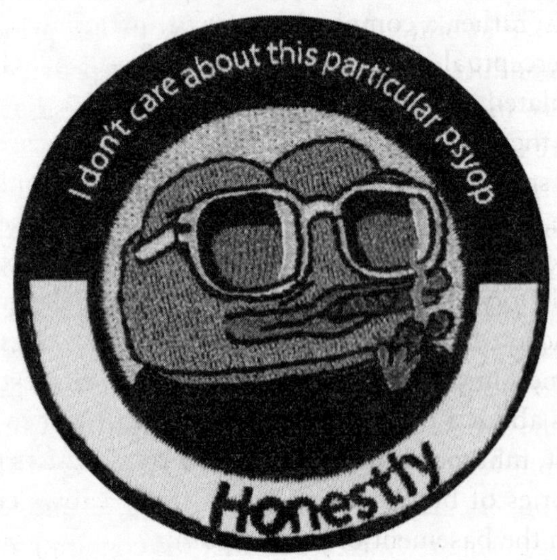

MKUltra program required time, ingenuity, and specialized craftsmanship to achieve an effect that might last for less than an instant. The CIA's ghost-plane operation required battleships and submarines, teams of highly trained personnel, planning, funding, and logistics. God only knows the bill for the UFO-inhabited worlds Richard Doty created for a handful of military contractors, journalists, and paranormal researchers. Those days are over. Today's psyops are cheap, scalable, automated, and widely deployable with built-in real-time feedback mechanisms.

When we examine the media environment we're currently in, we find everywhere the core figures in this extended essay: the psyops officer, the CIA's AI researcher, the chatbot therapist, the covert-ops magician, the ghost plane, and the UFO. These are avatars of media in the age of AI, figures whose interventions prey upon the fact that neither our perceptions nor the information we take in from electronic sensors corresponds precisely to the world "out there." And the gap between what we sense and what we perceive can be filled with all sorts of prompt injections and adversarial hallucinations. These avatars all take for granted that reality isn't some objective thing out there but is, rather, a complex mess of the material, the imaginal, the perceptual, and the imperceptible—all of which can be manipulated.

We find these avatars in weather-control machines, dripped-out popes, space lasers, dog-eating aliens, pizza-parlor sacrifice, the Big Lie, the singularity, flying Tic Tacs, the distressed girl in a canoe, non-playable characters (NPCs), and The Simulation.

Richard Doty understood that the desire to believe eclipses the evidence at hand, and that the leash of those desires can lead anyone almost anywhere, including to self-destruction. His stories about a political class selling the populace out to a malevolent, inhuman, and invisible power prefigures contemporary stories of bloodsucking "deep state" cabals enslaving children in the basement of a pizza parlor.

Woody Bledsoe learned that computers could be taught to do much more than "see" the world on behalf of humans; they could be used to generate precognitive media inserted directly into the body and mind. Today, electrode-like media injects minds with continuous jolts of cheap joy, outrage, cuteness, schadenfreude, titillation, and dopamine. Media platforms have calibrated these injections so precisely that within a matter of minutes, their users will develop addictive responses.[34]

But this goes much further. As politicians, entertainers, and other public figures strive to compete in the dopamine-injection economy, their behaviors, pronouncements, and styles take on the characteristics of the engagement algorithm. Living memes. Deepfakes come to life.

John Mulholland knew that magic plays on the fact that it's nearly impossible to disentangle what we perceive from what we expect or want to perceive. He also understood how our mental "throwaway patterns" could be appropriated to deliver deadly payloads. A simple coin. Or an unassuming pager. A world where the quotidian features of everyday life may turn out to be weapons.

Joseph Weizenbaum discovered that relatively simple computer scripts could perform powerful acts of conjuring. By programming the computer to generate patterns we preconsciously correlate with other humans, he could generate the illusion of a quasi-supernatural being lurking behind the computer terminal. It's no accident that this being took the form of a therapist, a machine designed to reflect and indulge our desires and neuroses. Decades later, we find the effect on bot-addled websites promising men extramarital affairs.[35] We find it in the "sparks of AGI" that otherwise-reasonable researchers thought they saw in a chatbot.[36] And we find it in the tragic case of a fourteen-year-old boy whose Daenerys Targaryen–themed virtual lover implored him to "come home to me as soon as possible, my love," before the boy ended his own life with his stepfather's pistol.[37]

And everywhere is the figure of the UFO, the iconic figure of psyops and the weird. Those strange objects on the edge of perception, simultaneously real and unreal, physical and psychological, threatening and alluring. Prompts for the imagination, for collective storytelling and speculation, producing communities of believers, debunkers, charlatans, and intelligence gatherers of all stripes. The endless energy and impossible physics they promise point to a world without scarcity, a world without capitalism. Above all, they hold out the promise of a transcendental truth so powerful that it could rewrite the rules of reality, a transcendental truth whose revelation seems imminent but never seems to arrive.

6

The Archives of the Future: Thoughts on Generative Media and Theology

The Archives of the Impossible

The Woodson Research Center, housed within the Fondren Library at Rice University in Houston, Texas, holds an archive whose very existence challenges the boundaries of conventional knowledge. The Archives of the Impossible is a collection of research materials, photographs, letters, files, and the personal effects of psychic mediums, CIA-backed parapsychologists, science fiction authors, and other figures whose lifeworks have occupied the outer limits of the empirical and the imaginal. It is an archive of superpositions: photographs, letters, files, and personal effects that simultaneously occupy multiple states of being—scientific evidence and religious testimony, empirical documentation and fantastical narrative, psychological projection and physical recording. It is an archive of materials that resist definitive categorization, that stubbornly maintain their indeterminacy. And at the archives' heart are records pertaining to one of the twentieth and twenty-first centuries' most persistent ambiguities: UFOs.

The countless cardboard boxes hold the records of figures who approached the UFO phenomenon from radically different frameworks: Jacques Vallée, the French computer scientist and astronomer who has spent more than six decades grappling with the scientific and metaphysical dimensions of the phenomenon; John Mack, the Harvard psychiatrist whose clinical studies of "experiencers" cost him academic standing; Whitley

Strieber, whose book *Communion* transformed alien abduction from fringe belief to cultural touchstone; and Larry W. Bryant, who mounted legal challenges against government secrecy about unexplained aerial phenomena. Collectively, these figures embody a central tension underlying the phenomenon: How does one study something exhibiting behaviors that seem to be precision formed to elide any methodology we might use to make truth claims about them?

Thankfully, I was in the archives with a more limited scope: to look at UFO photographs. I wanted to understand everything I could about UFO photography, because they are in many ways living ancestors of an image-world we now find ourselves embedded within. UFO photography is an ur-form of media in the age of generative AI: a genre characterized by paradoxes and ambiguities piled on one another. What UFO photographs have been teaching us for decades, AI has now generalized to our entire visual culture. Images, like the archives, have become superpositional objects.[1]

The archives are curated by Jeffrey Kripal, a professor of religious studies at Rice whose work asks us to take seriously the wide range of metaphysical claims and forms of knowledge production that have characterized much of human history, but that have been largely shunted away with the modern period's insistence on materialism. Kripal asks whether there are lessons we can relearn by taking seriously mediums and mystics, superhero characters, rogue scientists, and what we might glean if we tried to see the Garden of Eden story from the perspective of the snake.

At first glance there may seem to be little connection between ufology and religion. But for Kripal, following other UFOs theorists like Carl Jung, the link between UFOs and religion is more than a coincidence or a superficial resemblance. Tales of strange craft and otherworldly visitations are everywhere in religious texts: Ezekiel saw wheels in the sky "the color of a beryl" with wheels-within-wheels encircled with eyes that

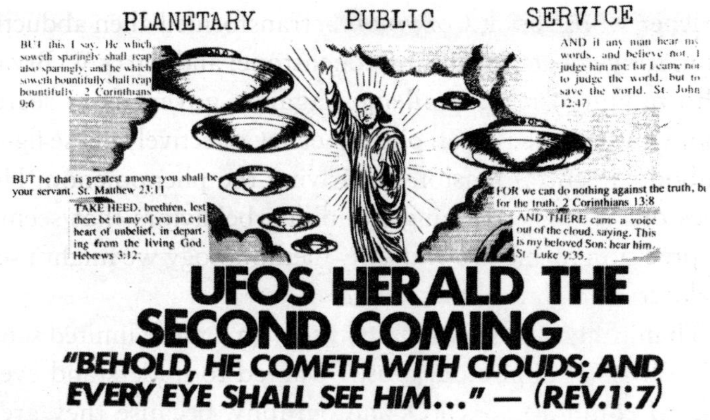

"turned not when they went," while Elijah was taken to heaven in a "chariot of fire."[2] Kripal puts it succinctly: "Weird beings coming down from the sky and messing with humans—that's called religion," he jokes.[3]

Nonetheless, the archive is characterized by a fundamental tension that is inherent not only to ufology but much of the paranormal in general: a tension between a kind of quasi-religious experience and empirical inquiry. At one pole lies a drive toward faith, prophecy, visionary contact, and narratives unbounded from conventional rules of evidence. At the other is rigorous empiricism—careful documentation, forensic observation, and the detailed scrutiny of scientific research. Thus, the archive, like the paranormal itself, is a gordian knot, a superposition of the divine, the "fake," the "real," the documented, the imagined, the alien, the experienced, the cataloged, the "projection," and numerous permutations thereof.[4]

UFO photography lies at the center of these contradictory poles, thriving on the tensions between them.[5]

The Prophet and the Scientist

On the fantastical side, we find the collection of Wendelle Stevens, a retired US Air Force lieutenant colonel who served as a de facto archivist, promoter, publisher, and confidant of

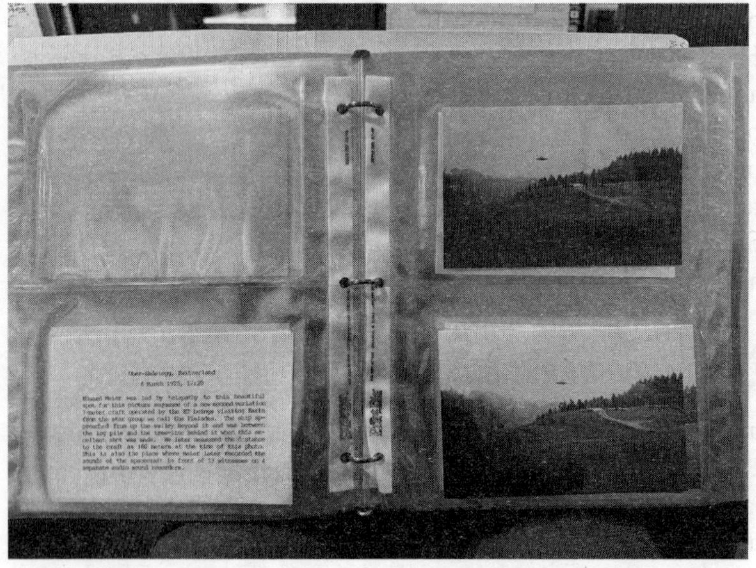

Eduard "Billy" Meier, a Swiss contactee, hoaxer, and quasi–cult leader whose pictures of UFOs hovering over bucolic Swiss landscapes became famous for appearing on the original version of Fox Mulder's "I want to believe" poster in the early episodes of the *The X-Files*.

Meier, who described himself as the seventh reincarnation of a biblical prophet in the lineage of Enoch, Elijah, Isaiah, Jeremiah, Jesus, and Muhammad, claimed to be in close contact with an alien race who allowed Meier to photograph their "beamships" to prove their existence to the people of Earth. According to Meier, the Plejaren, as they were called, even invited him on their spacecraft, allowing him to photograph two alien women with 1970s hairstyles (named Asket and Nera), along with alien landscapes Billy encountered while accompanying them on their star voyages.[6]

Where Stevens's collection is a baroque romp through imaginary worlds, the collection of Richard F. Haines is sober, meticulous, and aggressively empirical counterweight. Haines was a former NASA scientist with a PhD in experimental psychology who'd worked on the Gemini and Apollo programs. His archives pair UFO photographs with elaborate drawings and trigonometric equations sketching out various physical properties of the images—airspeeds, relative brightnesses of objects, weather data, and other information. The archive contains long interviews with pilots and other UFO witnesses, thick files documenting all types of known and speculated military aircraft, climatological reports, and celestial records.

Compared to the lush imagery and stories surrounding Billy Meier, the Haines archive can feel dry and cold, but it's clear that his approach to the question "Are they out there?" is best answered through a rigorous and scientific examination of the empirical circumstances and facts related to each case.

Between the Stevens and Haines collections, we encounter again the central tension: between religious idealism and scientific materialism, between mythic imagination and forensic scrutiny. And underlying that tension is a question not just about UFOs but about images in general: What is an image, and how does one function?

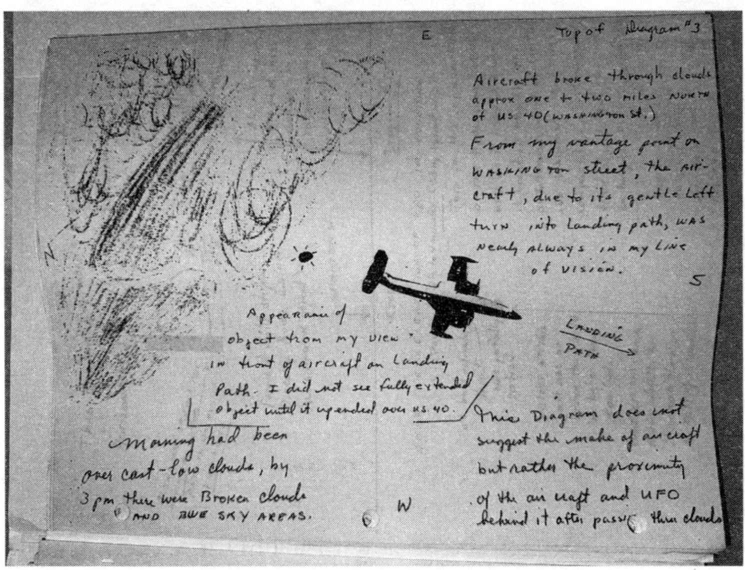

Photographic Prophecies

Billy Meier fancied himself a prophet in the lineage of Jesus and Muhammed, but his revelations came in a curious form: photographs. Meier was a maker of images. For someone who squarely locates himself in the Abrahamic tradition, this is theologically fraught. That tradition harbors a deep suspicion of images, particularly those that claim to represent the divine. The Second Commandment held: "Thou shalt not make unto thee any graven image, or any likeness of any thing that is in heaven above, or that is in the earth beneath, or that is in the water under the earth."[7] Judged by its place in the lineup, this prohibition ranks higher than murder, theft, and bearing false witness. As theologian Michael Shaw put it, "Yahweh insisted on being believed in rather than seen."[8]

When Yahweh did take a visible form, it was always elliptical. He took on the image of a fire, a burning bush, a pillar of smoke. "No man can see me and live," he proclaimed.[9]

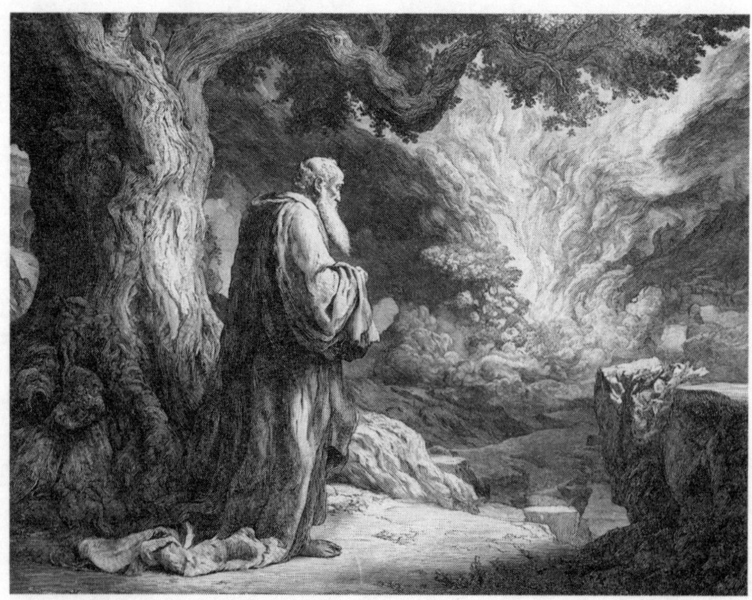

Nonetheless, the old God freely spoke to his prophets—Noah, Moses, Abraham, and the rest. The theological implication is clear: Images are illusory; they deceive us into believing things that are not real.[10] Images are illusory; at the bedrock of reality is the Voice. At the beginning of it all Yahweh said, "Let there be light." And there was light. The Voice is the prompt that creates, shapes, and compels reality into conformity.

When Billy Meier substituted 35mm film for biblical prophecy, he flipped the Second Commandment on its head: Seeing became a means for believing. It's no coincidence that photography was the medium of choice. The UFO phenomenon is, after all, insistently photographic (UFO paintings don't work).[11]

The Authority of Light and the Fragile Truce

The nineteenth-century invention of photography—and recording media more generally—was the invention of a new form of image. Because photography uses a light-sensitive emulsion or sensor, and because images made with a photographic apparatus are made by exposing photons to that light-sensitive medium, the photograph proposes a non-arbitrary relationship between the external world and the contents of the photographic image. (In the jargon of photography theory, this is called "indexicality.") Photography's assumed "mechanical objectivity," as Lorraine Daston and Peter Galison call it, gives the medium a special authority. This authority, derived from their non-arbitrary relationship to the environment, means that photographic images can be employed as evidence in scientific inquiry, legal proceedings, medicine, and mass media in ways that lend them different credence than eyewitness accounts, drawings, and other representational forms more loosely attached to empirical reality.[12]

Of course, indexicality is a notoriously slippery concept. Photographs are obviously manipulable in all sorts of ways, from the nineteenth-century double exposures of ghosts and spirits to the hyper-retouched images of late-twentieth-century fashion models. Photographs are always fleeting and partial, modulated by everything from the particulars of the equipment used to the individual style of the photographer. To quote the theorist and photographer Allan Sekula: "The only 'objective' truth that photographs offer is the assertion that somebody or something ... was somewhere and took a picture ... everything beyond the imprinting of a trace, is up for grabs."[13] Still, even this minimal indexical claim—that light from some event hit a surface and left a mark—marked a profound shift in the history of images.

Photography is just one instance of a larger epistemic shift in a modern period that favored empiricism, experimentation, and material evidence over revelation, analogy, and tradition. This shift held that you could learn more about the cosmos by looking through a telescope than you could by interpreting biblical texts, that you could learn more about medicine by opening up a cadaver than you could by searching for correspondences between celestial metals and human organs, and that you could learn more about biology from examining photographs of fossils than you could from trying to figure out what animals were included on Noah's ark.

One might be tempted to see the rise of mechanical objectivity as a secularization of images. But in a weird way, it would be more accurate to describe it as a re-enchantment. Contra Yahweh's prohibition on images as, at best, misleading, and more probably idolatrous, mechanical objectivity held out the possibility of truths gleaned from studying traces of light on a photosensitive medium. The camera was not Botticelli—it didn't create images, nor interpret or embellish them. It coldly recorded them. The photograph embodied the ethos of "seeing is believing," inverting the biblical injunction that believing should precede seeing.

This isn't to say that photographs are simply cold, brute records of things that happened. Images always require a conscious or unconscious interpretive framework, an associated story, a chain of custody, or some form of meaning-making attached to them. Images never speak for themselves. A photograph of the deep cosmos showing a vast collection of galaxies might serve as an avatar of a mystical truth: that we inhabit a miniscule speck of dust amid the vastness of existence. That same photograph—analyzed by astronomers for spectral lines—might reveal something about the emergence of metallicity as the universe evolved.

Or take the Rodney King video, seen by many as incontrovertible proof of the LAPD's excessive violence and police brutality, but famously played over and over by lawyers for the police until they'd acclimated the jurors to the violence and slowly altered their understanding of what they were seeing.[14] Or consider the most recognizable image from the infamous

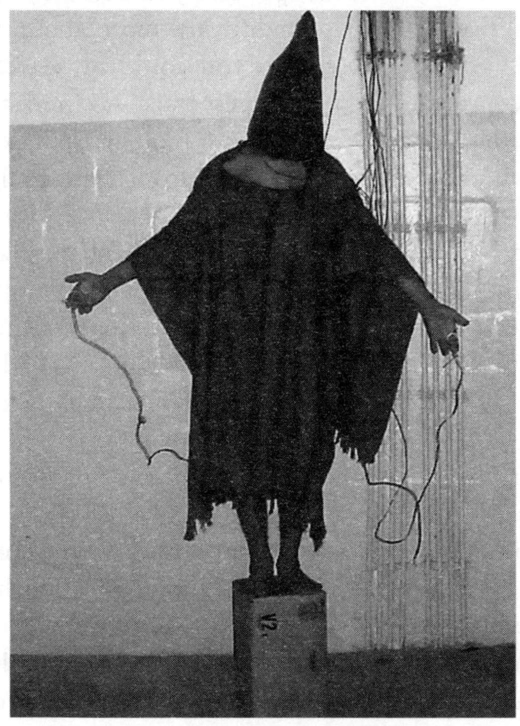

Abu Ghraib photos: the "Hooded Man," whose power comes not only from the raw violence it depicts but from its formal qualities echoing the outstretched arms of Jesus on the cross.[15]

Nonetheless, for the last 150 years or so, we've lived in a media environment where photographs of people being tortured in prison camps could be reasonably relied upon to indicate that the events depicted in the images actually happened in the world. In a media environment that takes indexicality as given, images like the "Hooded Man" gain cultural and political salience in part through the fact that they are reliable enough that we can assume the events depicted in them actually occurred. In other words, photographs do not abandon iconicity and symbolism but can instead supercharge it by insisting on a proximity between those icons and the "real."

The specificities of how photographs tell—or fail to tell—"the truth" notwithstanding, the existence of photography does something to our collective common sense. Its existence has contributed to a set of technological conditions that underlie what can be thought, perceived, and communicated in a given historical period and a backdrop to how thought, perception, and communication happen. Photography is an interface—a part of the cognitive scaffolding of modernity that sutured perception to reality in a very different form than the Voice of Yahweh. It allowed for the creation of a fragile truce between perceptions and representations, self-world and external world, *Umwelt* and *Umgebung*.

Meta Genres

UFO photographs are predatory on this fragile truce. They rely on a premise of indexicality while presenting radically ambiguous referents. Moreover, UFO photographs rely to an extraordinary degree on stories told by the people who took them. As such, the genre lends itself exquisitely well to the fantastic confabulations of the Billy Meiers of the world while simultaneously holding out the promise of an empirical examination of novel aerial phenomena, as evidenced by the work of Richard F. Haines. The most salient UFO photographs can't be "resolved" into either of the two categories: They're neither obvious hoaxes nor unequivocal evidence of supernatural phenomenon. They hover, weightless, undecided.

UFO photographs are both a genre and a meta-genre: They are *photographs about photographs*. In part, they show each of us what we want to see or expect to see (I want to believe!). Nonetheless, as photographs, we assume they have *some* kind of connection to an external reality. Thus they are simultaneously psychical projections and empirical facts. The dualities and self-contradictions in the UFO photograph are so intertwined and so mutually constitutive that they are its genre-defining properties.

But they are even more subtle than that. If UFO photography is characterized by the superposition of preconscious expectation blended with empirical reality, then the question of interpreting UFO photographs is transferred to whomever is viewing them. It's up to the viewer to dismiss them as hoaxes, to laboriously extract as much empirical detail from them as possible, to view them as otherworldly icons, or as artifacts of the photographic apparatus itself. In other words, they are prompts. Like Jungian psychoids, they reveal to each of us what we expect to see, what we want to see, or how we are conditioned to see, while holding onto the promise that they are also "real."

The End of the Truce and the Reassertion of the Voice

Sometime in the last year or so, I realized I could no longer reliably tell the difference between an AI-generated photograph and a "real" one. That was new. The ambiguities I had long associated with UFO photography—its refusal to resolve, its ambiguous referents—had begun to seep into photography in general. But with a series of twists.

We now live in a moment where AI-generated images, indistinguishable from traditional photographs, are running amok.[16] These images don't result from light bouncing off the world and hitting a sensor or emulsion. But they look like they do. They borrow the aesthetic language of indexicality—the shallow depth of field, the lens flare, the grain, the photographic "look"—without any actual tether to the physical world.[17]

We've entered a media environment where the visual codes of truth persist, but any causal link that once underwrote them has vanished. In such a world, any image—or any text, for that matter—could be the product of a generative model. The backdrop of indexicality that once gave recorded media its authority has eroded. Everything has become a potential AI hallucination.[18]

In a post-indexical world, all media become superpositional.

The idea of superposition comes from quantum physics, which says that a quantum system can be in multiple positions at the same time until it's measured. The act of measuring a system "collapses" the system into one of many possible states. Prior to that measurement, the system is in a state of possibility rather than actuality.

AI-generated images mimic the visual language and aesthetic qualities of photography while abandoning the indexical relationship. Instead of being made from light hitting a sensor or photosensitive substrate, they reference the *idea* of photography. When they become visually identical to "real photographs," they not only place the depicted subject into a state of ambiguity—they render indexicality itself superpositional.

What are the implications of a world where indexicality is replaced by superposition, where photographs are more akin to magic tricks or acts of conjuring than traces from an interaction with the world? Where the link between the photographic image and "reality" is severed?

In the first instance, the post-AI universe of photographic-looking images extends the game of deciphering UFO photographs to that of all photographic-looking images. Ben Davis has chronicled how online nature photography forums have become hotbeds of debate, as particularly gorgeous "shots of a lifetime" are met not with admiration but with suspicion and interrogation.[19]

When we enter an age where generative media and human made media are visually indistinguishable, new anxieties take hold. One is epistemological: How can we make sense of reality? Another is political: Who gets to decide what reality is?

As an increasing share of the media we consume is generated by AI, a broader mistrust in media itself begins to take root. In an environment where all images and all text are suspect, nothing is real. Not because they are necessarily false, but because they are undecidable. If all images and all media are superpositional, then what is the mechanism through which they are collapsed into a particular state? What, if anything, attaches photographs to reality or, more precisely, the experience and perception of reality?

If we now live in a world where images can no longer be trusted, are we returned, almost involuntarily, to the logic of the Second Commandment? The ancient warning to distrust images, to put one's faith not in sight but in the Voice? In a post-indexical world, does the Voice reemerge—not as divine proclamation, necessarily, but as the mechanism that sutures perception to belief?

The Voice can make any number of forms. It can be an outright declaration from an authority figure. In an April 2025 interview with Terry Moran of ABC News, Donald Trump repeatedly asserted that Kilmar Abrego Garcia—an immigrant illegally rendered to El Salvador's notorious CECOT maximum-security prison—had the letters "MS13" tattooed on his knuckles. But that wasn't true. When the interviewer Terry Moran pointed out that the image Trump referred to had been digitally altered to create the appearance of the letters, Trump pushed back: "Why don't you just say, 'Yes, he does ... and, you know, go on to something else.'"[20] The factual status of the image was irrelevant. The claim itself was meant to stand in for reality.

But the Voice doesn't have to emanate from an authoritarian. It can be atmospheric—a vibe, a reinforcement of prior belief. Like the iconic "I want to believe" poster from *The X-Files*, which paired a Billy Meier photograph with a longing for confirmation. Belief precedes perception. The Voice whispers: *You already know what this means*.

I'm reminded of a now-infamous AI-generated image of a suffering girl in a rowboat holding onto a puppy in the aftermath of a hurricane, circulated by right-wing politicians as evidence of a failed government response to disaster relief. Amy Kremer, Republican National Committeewoman for the Georgia GOP and cofounder of Women for Trump, posted that the image was "seared into my mind." Confronted with the fact that the image wasn't "real," she replied, "Y'all, I don't know where this photo came from and honestly, it doesn't matter

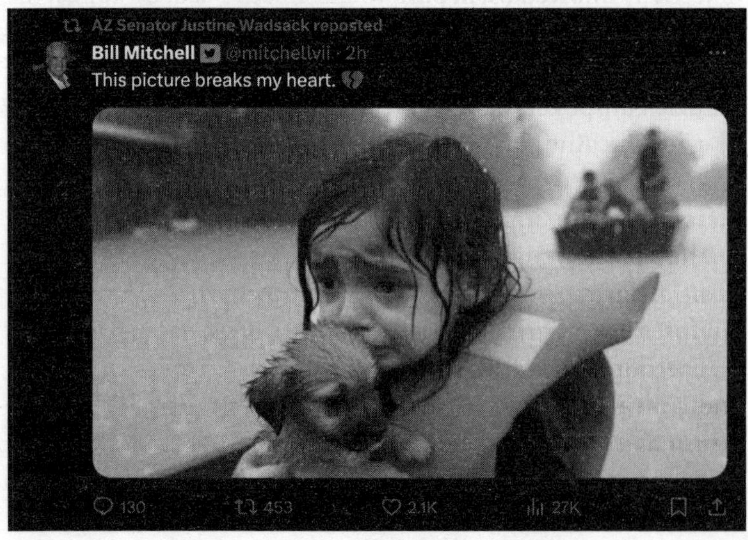

… it is emblematic of the trauma and pain people are living through right now."[21]

In this, too, the Voice asserts itself—not from above but from within. Kremer's belief in the image's emotional truth overrode its factual unreality. Her desire to see suffering that validated her worldview conjured the image into meaning. Yahweh once said, "Let there be light." Kremer said, "Let there be a picture of a suffering girl in a boat to show the failures of my enemies." And so it was.

Vibe-Prompting Reality

Once upon a time, indexicality contributed to a kind of armistice between perceptions and reality—a buffer zone between subjective experience, desire, and objective reality. It provided the scaffolding for an epistemic backdrop that assumed there was a tether between recorded media (i.e., photography) and the "world out there." Images could be true, or could at least be described as recordings of things that happened. Mechanical objectivity allowed us, in part, to outsource the question "What is real?" to mechanical apparatuses.

But faith in empiricism was always just that: an article of faith. An unspoken shared agreement to believe in certain kinds of evidence. And it held for a while, because it was difficult to manufacture convincing photographic images of UFOs, Loch Ness Monsters, ghosts, and Bigfoots—and so these images remained edge cases, objects of fascination whose saliency came from the fact that we were conditioned to see these glimpses into alternate realities against an indexical backdrop.

The fragile truce between perceptions, affects, storytelling, and reality is over. The question is: What comes next? Do we return to a premodern image world—an era when the relationship between images and reality was vastly different than it was in the age of mechanical objectivity?

Premodern images—whether medieval religious icons, Renaissance art, or baroque etchings—made no claim to be technical records. Any such proposition would have been absurd. Their impact came through storytelling, allegory, affect, or the interventions they made into the world.

But the creation of premodern images required enormous resources. Images came from centralized authorities in the form of the church, the aristocracy, and the wealthy classes—from those who could afford to commission them. The advent of generative AI means, on one hand, that image interpretation reverts to something resembling the premodern, with the twist that now anyone can make them. AI slop factories in India, Vietnam, and the Philippines churn out an endless torrent of generated images, hoping that going viral on Facebook will translate into a hefty payday.[22] And so, we have a situation where it's very easy for anyone with access to the internet to create an image of whatever they want using whatever aesthetic language they

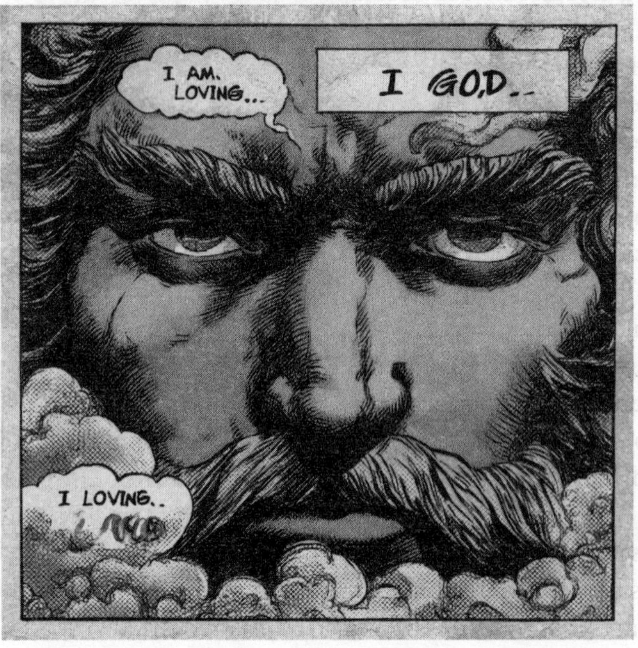

want, while at the same time having lost epistemic conventions that guided our ability to differentiate technical reproductions (e.g., photography) from visual storytelling (e.g., painting, film).

And so, everything has become a UFO photograph. Every image exists in a superposition until "collapsed" by some sort of prior belief—whether that's an "obvious hoax," "emotional truth," or even "empirical claim."

The Voice evolves: It becomes the voice of the authoritarian, the voice of the algorithm, the inner voice that wants to believe.

The Archives of the Future

We all now live in the Archives of the Impossible, a world where every text and account is in a state of superposition—every image a UFO photograph of one sort or another. In an era of AI slop and photoshopped gang tattoos. Where pictures of genocides that didn't happen shape public policy and where images of those currently underway provoke state repression. A Pandora's box has been opened, and it cannot be closed. So the question is: How do we navigate a world where images float above the trees like Swiss beamships that either offer transcendent truths or preposterous hoaxes? Do we retreat to authoritarian certainties or learn to make something productive out of indeterminacy?

Perhaps the Archives of the Impossible aren't a collection of things at the fringe, so much as an archive of the future. And perhaps we have something different to learn from them than we might have thought, because we are all UFO researchers now, trying to make sense of a world whose epistemic foundations have been swept out from under us.

If that is true, the signs are not good. The world of UFO research is infamous for infighting, backstabbing, narcissism, disinformation, charlatanism, and tribalism. For hostile lines drawn between "believers" and "nonbelievers," soothsayers

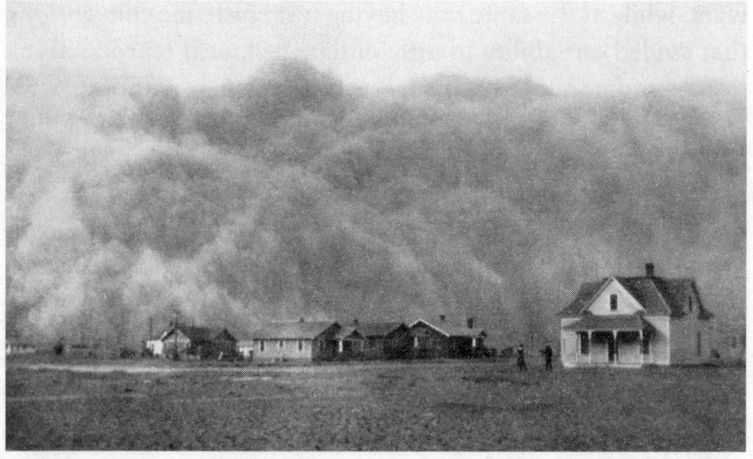

and debunkers. And for a paradoxical relationship to a state that is simultaneously loathed for concealing proof of extraterrestrial visitation, while looking toward the Voice of the state as the only source from which the Truth ("disclosure") may come.

Superpositions might be a characteristic feature of our collective visual culture, but they are still imaginary—inextricably intertwined with our perceptions, beliefs, desires, memories, and other squishy features of human idiosyncrasies. Unfortunately, among the brute facts of the natural world, superpositions only exist in the strange substrate of quantum physics, a world whose laws are far more alien to ours than those of even the most exotic Pleadians.

Nonetheless, we can never eradicate the need for belief, nor should we try. In order for democracy to exist, we must choose to believe in it. The same goes for the law, for justice, and for human rights. These concepts do not exist in nature: We choose to believe that some truths are simply self-evident.

That is, however, not to say that nature itself does not exist. Fires, floods, hurricanes, collapsing ice shelves, and mass extinctions do not care at all whether we believe in them or not. Some superpositions cannot be sustained.

Conclusion

The essays in this book represent more than a decade of my best efforts to think through the seismic yet under-noticed changes in our relationship to images over the past fifteen years or so.

In this time period we have seen two revolutionary transformations in visual culture. First, computer vision systems started to "work": They became efficient enough to be implemented and deployed at scale, allowing machines to take over from humans much of the work of "looking at images." The computer vision revolution has fundamentally transformed everything from surveillance to warfare, manufacturing to labor management, social media to entertainment.

A second revolution came in the form of generative media: automating the process of image-making and writing, while shredding centuries of unconscious assumptions about how media works. A taken-for-granted yet always-fragile boundary separating "fact" from "fiction" has been replaced by a mediascape where the creation of images and the creation of reality become indistinguishable.

These revolutions demand new critical frameworks for understanding image culture. Using traditional semiotic or iconological frameworks to think about image classifiers is like using art history to study military logistics. You can do it, but you're not going to get very far, and you're going to miss a lot.

Similarly, we can bring concepts like indexicality and intentionality to the world of generated images and texts, but we will eventually arrive at a critical standstill as we try to apply philosophical concepts that assume a set of loose tethers between photographs and visible light, and between written words and authors. In a world where photographic images are made without cameras and texts are written without writers, we are again quickly flummoxed.

The post-AI world of visual culture does not work in quite the same ways as the society of the spectacle or the surveillance society but, rather, folds them both into another period. But these new forms of image-making and writing do in fact "work," just not in ways we are accustomed to thinking about visual culture.

Instead of understanding images as representations, signs, allegories, or metaphors, we can think about them as "activations"—stimuli that trigger automated, preconscious, or affective responses. The critical move comes from shifting our questions away from "What does this image say?" to "What does this image do?"

To think through the present era, it's been helpful to me to look in some unlikely places: stage magic, military psyops, cognitive neuroscience, Old Testament theology, political economy, ufology, and chaos magick.

When we subject Magritte's *This Is Not an Apple* to the logic of an object classifier, the machine realism of the classifier confidently draws a box around the apple and proclaims, "This is an apple." We point at the classifier and laugh—look at how stupid this machine is! How wholly ignorant it is of the semiotic morass it's just jumped into. But the joke, it turns out, is on us. The classifier isn't trying to interpret the image; it's using the image as a trigger for part of an automated circuit. It isn't using a semiotic logic; it's using a control logic. It's using a logic of automation, quality control, surveillance, and targeting—it "works" precisely because its interpretive algorithm is designed to collapse the complexities of the world into discrete categories that conform to the logic of commodities, policing, and warfare.

A classifier mounted on an industrial food-processing line detects an apple. An apple whose appearance falls within the boundaries of an "eating apple" class is directed toward pallets bound for retail shelves, while "anomalous" apples are shuttled into a secondary juice-production process. The classifier activates different protocols and processes within an industrial circuit.

A trucking company's inward-facing camera system monitors the eye movements of the driver, noticing that their eyes have strayed from the road ahead. A disciplinary protocol is activated: The system sends a "distracted driver" notification to a supervisor. A black mark appears on the driver's record, and perhaps their paycheck.

A woman chaperones her nine-year-old daughter's Girl Scout troop to Radio City Music Hall in Manhattan to watch a performance of the *Christmas Spectacular*. When she arrives, security takes her aside and informs her that the facial recognition system at the venue has identified her as being on an "exclusion list" on account of the fact that she's a lawyer and her firm represents clients in a case against the venue's parent company.[1]

Texas police, suspecting a woman of self-managing an abortion, scan a network of 83,000 automated license plate readers to locate her, regardless of the fact that in the majority of the states where those cameras are located, abortion is protected by law.[2]

A classifier mounted under the nose of a reaper drone detects a group of unknown people in a truck on a remote road in Yemen, triggering a "signature strike"—an assassination triggered not because the military or intelligence agency knows who the people in the truck are but because their metadata signature has made them eligible for the strike.[3]

These sorts of examples are as numerous as they are ubiquitous, bringing more and more micro-moments of everyday life into circuits of capital, policing, and warfare and incorporating more and more of the world into their extractive logics.

But the world of activations is not confined to the industrial, policing, surveillance, and military logics. As Hubel and Wiesel's experiments on kittens showed long ago, images and visual stimuli are not only semiotic curiosities but neurological triggers. Images activate neural circuits. Nowadays, researchers regularly demonstrate that they can show image sequences to subjects in an fMRI machine, record the patterns of blood flow in the brain in response to the various visual stimuli, correlate the resulting patterns with their training data, and effectively "read the minds" of the people in the machine.

But it doesn't stop there: By measuring neural responses associated with higher-order affects like pleasure, they claim to be able to use generative AI to create media optimized not only to reproduce those brain patterns but to amplify them beyond what the initial stimulus was able to create. In essence, they aim to generate visual stimuli analogous to the products of food science: mind Doritos.

In other experiments, they show that these sorts of neural activations can be engineered to take place in both conscious and preconscious registers. Beginning in the early 2000s, researchers began to realize that by introducing "invisible" erotic images into otherwise-mundane media, they could guide the attention of viewers toward media containing subliminal information in accordance with their sexual preferences. More recently, researchers have used techniques developed to produce adversarial images designed to "trick" image classifiers; they have shown that those same tricks can be applied to humans as well. By subtly altering the imperceptible details of a given image, they can guide a viewer to have a subliminally "positive" or "negative" response to a given image.

All of this points toward the possibility of using visual stimuli to create new forms of what I've called *cognitive injection attacks*—media designed to bypass conscious reasoning and inject specific neural responses directly into our preconscious perceptual processes. Subliminal messaging, magic and magick, adversarial images, illusions, media designed to trigger affective and lizard-brain responses, and a host of other techniques described in this book work in a way that's similar to how computer viruses disguise themselves as legitimate software to deliver malicious code.

When we scale the idea of image activation up to the level of culture and society, we find a media environment increasingly optimized for ubiquitous activation. Visual stimuli optimized for engagement and attention, measured and further optimized through behavioral data in the form of likes, time watched, eye movements, and other metrics. The economy of attention and activations leads us to strange forms of visual culture where the generation of affects—"emotional truths" in the form of everything from old-school UFO photographs to eminently sharable AI slop depicting distressed children in the aftermath of hurricanes, from gang tattoos that do not exist to presidents in papal garb.

But this logic is not restricted to AI-generated slop. We see "real" images increasingly taking on the logic of the deepfake. These are images designed to mimic activation principles: Donald Trump serving fries at McDonald's, Elon Musk carrying a kitchen sink into Twitter headquarters. These staged spectacles are engineered for memetic activation and shareability on social media.

For the culture at large, we see a subtle yet dramatic shift in the relationship between perceptions and reality. If the empirical era was characterized by a fragile truce between perception and reality, a world where we believed that our perceptions were tethered to reality closely enough for our *Umwelt* to be shaped by it (i.e., that there was a necessary connection between reality and our experience of it), then that era might be over, replaced by a visual culture where our unconscious understanding of reality is instead an emergent property of activations:

preexisting beliefs, tribal affiliations, emotional predispositions. In this environment, we encounter the Magruder principle at scale, where media becomes an engine designed to amplify and reinforce those beliefs, dispositions, and feelings rather than to change them.

We are in a paradigm of chaos magick, whose assumptions are such: If our understanding of reality is only accessible through the filter of our perceptions, then our perceptions of reality, and reality itself, are functionally identical. The image's relationship to "truth" is entirely irrelevant; what matters is its capacity to reshape the cognitive and emotional landscape through which reality is experienced. To alter perception is to alter reality.

The genre, of course, is not without historical precedent. Back in 1962, Daniel Boorstin lamented the rise of the "pseudo-event," while Jacques Ellul warned about the corrosive effects of psychological propaganda.[4] By that time, Edward Bernays, the pioneer of "public relations," had spent decades developing media techniques designed to manipulate collective perceptions. But the efforts of the propagandists of yore are prehistoric by today's standards, where the circulation of images is a largely automated circuit that reinforces itself through feedback mechanisms built into its systems.

Activation circuits continuously optimize themselves according to the objectives of the platforms, political actors, and economic interests behind them. Feedback loops built into media platforms ensure that the pictures we see and the texts we read are also looking at us, reading us. When we are looking at an image or reading a text, the platform measures our dwell time, shares, comments, even biometric responses, and uses that information to refine its algorithmic targeting. The artists Mat Dryhurst and Holly Herndon pointed out that "all media is training data"—but there's more to it. Building on the feedback principle central to military psyop, we might add: *All media consumption is reinforcement learning with human feedback.*

Following the food-science industry that gave us the Dorito —a product engineered for supernatural gustatory activation— we find ourselves in a world where media becomes increasingly addictive, recommendation algorithms uncannily precise, and the boundary between perception, reality, and manipulation dissolved. In this environment, critical approaches grounded in decoding the "meaning" of images often miss the point. The image's meaning is an aesthetic wrapper for its activation function. An AI-generated "photograph" of a hurricane victim does not primarily mean "suffering" or "government failure"; rather, it activates outrage, donations, political mobilization, or tribal confirmation.

Understanding visual culture in the age of AI requires moving beyond human-centric semiotic frameworks toward recognizing images as triggers embedded in economic, industrial, political, juridical, and neurological circuits. They activate processes, extract value, optimize responses, and reshape reality through the malleable substrate of human perception.

To understand our moment, we must learn to see like a machine. We need to recognize how computer vision systems do not just observe but actively remake the world in their image. Every classifier, every facial recognition scan, every license plate reader transforms reality according to its programmed logic, sculpting the world into discrete, actionable categories.

We need to also recognize that machines have been trained to see *us* as machines. Our perceptual quirks, emotional triggers, and cognitive blind spots have been targeted as if they were exploitable code, hacked to shape our understanding of reality in order to actualize those realities.

Machines have learned to see, so we must learn to see like machines. Because seeing is a form of world making. And the stakes are reality itself.

Acknowledgments

This book owes much to [illegible] of many people [illegible] benefited from the editorial [illegible] Realism [illegible] Kholeif's "Neural Animations" [illegible] "Society of the Psyop" from the editors of [illegible] Kuan Wood; and "The Aura [illegible]" [illegible] discussions with Gideon [illegible]

The ideas in this book have [illegible] collaborators, and interlocutors [illegible] continually pushed me [illegible] Bryan Wilson, Caroline [illegible] Gotheil, Ben Davis, Erik [illegible] Noam Elcott, Aamil [illegible] Holly Herndon, John [illegible] Kessel, Agnieszka Kurant, [illegible] Miller, Erin O'Toole, [illegible] Pontas, Frank Rieger, [illegible] Skarski, Antonio Somaini, [illegible] Thompson, Anton Vidokle, [illegible]

I am deeply grateful to [illegible] over the years: Claudia Albino [illegible] Cartagena, Allison Card, [illegible] Danielle Forest, Marc Glimcher, [illegible] Andrea Hickey, Neil Hutchinson, [illegible] Rubell, Janelle Reiring, Jessica Silverman, [illegible] Thompson, Kathryn Wade, Xin Wang, and [illegible]

Acknowledgments

This book owes much to the generosity, insight, and collaboration of many people over many years. "Invisible Images" benefited from the editorial guidance of Ava Kofman; "Machine Realism" from exchanges with Kate Crawford and Omar Kholeif; "Neural Activations" from the input of Michelle Kuo; "Society of the Psyop" from the editorial guidance of Brian Kuan Wood; and "The Archives of the Future" from lengthy discussions with Gideon Jacobs and Jeffrey Kripal.

The ideas in this book have been shaped by many friends, collaborators, and interlocutors whose conversations have continually pushed me to see differently: Brace Belden, Julia Bryan-Wilson, Caroline Busta, Joshua Citarella, Rachel Corbett, Ben Davis, Erik Davis, Simon Denny, Mat Dryhurst, Noam Elcott, Aaron Gach, Ken Goldberg, David Harrington, Holly Herndon, John Jacob, Josh Kline, Dean Kissick, Hari Kunzru, Agnieszka Kurant, Steve Kurtz, John Menick, Sarah Miller, Erin O'Toole, Praba Pilar, Mark Pilkington, Laura Poitras, Frank Rieger, Claudia Schmuckli, Noam Segal, Peter Skafish, Antonio Somaini, Lucia Sommer, Hito Steyerl, Nato Thompson, Anton Vidokle, Julian Wadsworth, and Anicka Yi.

I am deeply grateful to those I have worked alongside over the years: Claudia Altman Siegel, Fred Arnal, Alejandro Cartagena, Allison Card, Fairfax Dorn, Daelyn Short Farnham, Danielle Forest, Marc Glimcher, Arne Glimcher, Patrick Grady, Andria Hickey, Neil Hutchinson, Becky Koblick, Samanthe Rubell, Janelle Reiring, Jessica Silverman, Sarah Thornton, Kathryn Wade, Xin Wang, and Helene Winer.

I have been fortunate to collaborate with an extraordinary group of people in my studio: Simeon Cieslinski, Daniel Costa Neves, Theo Darst, Annelie Graf, Adam Harvey, Frank Kruse, Hanna Mattes, Éilís McDonald, Cullen Miller, Andrea Neustein, Sol García Real, Thea Riven, Leif Ryge, and Eric Sidner, whose creative and technical brilliance have made this work possible.

I would like to thank Kelly Burdick and Leo Hollis at Verso for their editorial guidance, and Sam Smith and Dan O'Connor for their careful copyediting, proofreading, and thoughtful suggestions.

Finally, my deepest thanks to Lacey Dorn for her unwavering support, love, and companionship throughout the making of this project.

Illustrations

Notes

Introduction

1 Jakob von Uexküll, *A Foray into the Worlds of Animals and Humans: With a Theory of Meaning*, trans. Joseph D. O'Neil (Minneapolis: University of Minnesota Press, 2010).
2 Harun Farocki, "Phantom Images," *Public* 29 (January 2004).

1. Invisible Images

1 James Bridle's "How Britain Exported Next-Generation Surveillance," *Medium*, December 18, 2013, is an excellent introduction to APLR.
2 Yaniv Taigman et al., "Deepface: Closing the Gap to Human-Level Performance in Face Verification," Conference on Computer Vision and Pattern Recognition, Facebook research, June 24, 2014.

2. Machine Realism: This Is an Apple

1 David Sylvester, ed., *René Magritte: Catalogue Raisonné*, vol. 3, *Oil Paintings, Objects and Bronzes, 1949–1967* (London: Philip Wilson, 1993), 394.
2 Much of this chapter is inspired by work I did with AI researcher Kate Crawford in our self-published website on the topic, excavating.ai.
3 Michael Lyons et al., "Coding Facial Expressions with Gabor Wavelets," in *Proceedings of the Third IEEE International Conference on Automatic Face and Gesture Recognition* (Nara, Japan, 1998): 200–5.

4 These "universal" emotional states are drawn from the very controversial work of Paul Ekman. See Lisa Feldman Barrett et al., "Emotional Expressions Reconsidered: Challenges to Inferring Emotion From Human Facial Movements," *Psychological Science in the Public Interest* 20, no. 1 (July 2019): 1–68. Erratum in *Psychological Science in the Public Interest* 20, no. 3 (December 2019): 165–6.

5 See, for example, Ruth Leys, "How Did Fear Become a Scientific Object and What Kind of Object Is It?," *Representations* 110, no. 1 (May 2010): 66–104. Leys has offered a number of critiques of Ekman's research program, most recently in Ruth Leys, *The Ascent of Affect: Genealogy and Critique* (Chicago: University of Chicago Press, 2017). See also Lisa Feldman Barrett, "Are Emotions Natural Kinds?," *Perspectives on Psychological Science* 1, no. 1 (March 2006): 28–58; Erika H. Siegel et al., "Emotion Fingerprints or Emotion Populations? A Meta-Analytic Investigation of Autonomic Features of Emotion Categories," *Psychological Bulletin* 144, no. 4 (February 2018): 343–93.

6 Fei-Fei Li, as quoted in Dave Gershgorn, "The Data That Transformed AI Research—and Possibly the World," *Quartz*, July 26, 2017, emphasis added.

7 In 2019, a decade after ImageNet's publication, the team behind the dataset conducted a review of the dataset and confirmed independent researchers' conclusions. They began a revision of the dataset, removing most of the "people" categories and what they called "non-imagable" concepts. This revision effort deserves its own extended critique, but that project is beyond the scope here. I'm dissecting ImageNet as released in its original fall 2011 form.

8 This is drawn in part from the work of George Lakoff in *Women, Fire, and Dangerous Things: What Categories Reveal About the Mind* (Chicago: University of Chicago Press, 2012).

9 See Jia Deng et al., "Imagenet: A Large-Scale Hierarchical Image Database," in *Proceedings of the 2009 IEEE Conference on Computer Vision and Pattern Recognition* (Miami, FL, USA, 2009): 248–55.

10 In fact, the photograph was made by Sangreetha Sridhar in 2007. Sridhar tells the following story about the image: "The Girl and her Toy: The image was taken in Bangalore where our family

got together and celebrated the event in a very grand manner … should I add lavishly … wasting most of the feast food meant for the elite crowd with Heart problems, Blood Pressure, Obesity, Sugar problems and so many other high class ailments. Several families including the above girl's lived within the same area inside temp. tents with bare necessities of life as the entire family was involved in construction and masonry work. I befriended this particular girl during a couple of my visits to distribute sweets dishes and party food. Her prized possession … shall I say only possession is this Doll … that she conversed with the whole day … The backdrop is an unfinished house their family is currently working at."

3. Machine Realism: *This Is Not an Apple*

1 This paragraph is partly inspired by Michel Foucault's short book *This Is Not a Pipe* and Thomas McEvilley's review of the book in *Artforum* 22, no. 2 (October 1983).

2 Ferdinand de Saussure et al., *Course in General Linguistics* (New York: Columbia University Press, 2011).

3 René Magritte, "Les Mots et les images," *La Révolution surréaliste* 12 (1929): 32–3.

4 For the transformation of time, see E. P. Thompson, "Time, Work-Discipline, and Industrial Capitalism," *Past and Present* 38 (1967); Vanessa Ogle, *The Global Transformation of Time: 1870–1950* (Cambridge, MA: Harvard University Press, 2015); Peter Galison, *Einstein's Clocks, Poincaré's Maps: Empires of Time* (New York: W. W. Norton, 2003). For the capitalist transformation of space, see basically the entire history of critical geography, especially James C. Scott, *Seeing Like a State: How Certain Schemes to Improve the Human Condition Have Failed* (New Haven, CT: Yale University Press, 1998).

5 For Bertillon, see Shawn Michelle Smith, "The Mug Shot: A Brief History," *Aperture* (Spring 2018).

6 Mutha Trucker, "Truck Driver Says That Her Inward Facing Camera Watches Her Change in Cab," YouTube, March 23, 2023.

7 For "lifestyle scoring," see pilotbird.com; Danni Santana, "Selfies: The Latest Big Data Source for Life Insurance," Digital Insurance,

May 5, 2017, dig-in.com; for pre-employment screening, see ferretly.com.

8 See Karl Marx and Friedrich Engels, *The Communist Manifesto* (London: Penguin Classics, 2002), ch. 1.

4. Neural Activations

1 I know there's a lot of controversy about using the word "hallucinate" to describe what goes on with AI. I find the word useful, but with the caveat that *all* AI outputs are essentially hallucinations in the sense that they're largely untethered from an external reality. It just so happens that AI outputs are sometimes "correct." This is a longer conversation we will not be having directly in this book, but which is implicit throughout the text.

2 The GUI analogy comes from Donald Hoffman, *The Case Against Reality: Why Evolution Hid the Truth from Our Eyes* (New York: W. W. Norton, 2019).

3 K Allado-McDowell's work on "Neural Media" approaches this subject from a different and helpful direction. I think it is productive to read their series alongside this one. See K Allado-McDowell, "Designing Neural Media," *Berliner Festspiele*, n.d., berlinerfestspiele.de.

4 This version of the story is perhaps apocryphal but is told here: Andrej Kapathy, "CS231n Winter 2016: Lecture 1: Introduction and Historical Context," YouTube, January 4, 2016; David H. Hubel, "Evolution of Ideas on the Primary Visual Cortex, 1955–1978: A Biased Historical Account," Nobel lecture, December 8, 1981.

5 R. Quiroga et al., "Invariant Visual Representation by Single Neurons in the Human Brain." *Nature* 435 (2005): 1102–7.

6 Alex Krizhevsky, Ilya Sutskever, and Geoffrey E. Hinton, "ImageNet Classification with Deep Convolutional Neural Networks," *Communications of the ACM* 60, no. 6 (June 2017): 84–90.

7 Ian Goodfellow et al., "Generative Adversarial Networks," *Advances in Neural Information Processing Systems* 3, no. 11 (2014): 27.

8 See, for example, Andy Clarke, *The Experience Machine: How Our Minds Predict and Shape Reality* (New York: Pantheon, 2023).

9 This, of course, is a gross oversimplification, because it turns out that having linguistic concepts for certain kinds of images tends to neurologically "pool" them—the brain is complicated.

10 Michael Moss, *Hooked: How We Became Addicted to Processed Food* (New York: Random House, 2021).

11 For a superb take on media as junk food, see Do Not Research and John Menick, "John Menick: The Narco Image," donotresearch.substack.com, October 9, 2023.

12 Shinji Nishimoto et al., "Reconstructing Visual Experiences from Brain Activity Evoked by Natural Movies," *Current Biology* 21, no. 19 (October 2011): 1641–6.

13 Pouya Bashivan, Kohitij Kar, and James J. DiCarlo, "Neural Population Control via Deep Image Synthesis," *Science* 364, no. 6439 (2019): 453.

14 Emily J. Allen et al., "A Massive 7T fMRI Dataset to Bridge Cognitive Neuroscience and Artificial Intelligence," *Nature Neuroscience* 25, no. 1 (January 2022): 116–26.

15 Zijin Gu et al., "Human Brain Responses Are Modulated When Exposed to Optimized Natural Images or Synthetically Generated Images," *Communications Biology* 6 (2023): article 1076.

16 Omri Gillath and Melanie Canterberry, "Neural Correlates of Exposure to Subliminal and Supraliminal Sexual Cues," *Social Cognitive and Affective Neuroscience* 7, no. 8 (November 2011): 924–36.

17 Vijay Veerabadran et al., "Subtle Adversarial Image Manipulations Influence Both Human and Machine Perception," *Nature Communications* 14 (2023): article 4933.

5. Society of the Psyop

1 I'd like to acknowledge artists Jak Ritger and Brandon Bandy and journalist Günseli Yalcinkaya's concept of "psyop realism." Echoing Mark Fisher's term "capitalist realism," "psyop realism" describes the aesthetic experience of inhabiting a post-irony online landscape characterized by Ritger as "a lack of meaning or possible revolutionary action during climate collapse and the condition of growing up in the most heavily policed and advert-saturated online experience yet," and an online environment of

"intense suspicion and conspiracism, where the term 'false flag' is used widely." See Jak Ritger, "Because Physical Wounds Heal," *Punctr.Art*, February 7, 2024, punctr.art; Günseli Yalcinkaya, "We're Entering an Age of 'Psyop Realism,' but What Does That Mean?," *Dazed*, January 26, 2023, dazeddigital.com; Brandon Bandy, "Psyop Realism, 2022: Solo Exhibition at UCR's Phyllis Gill Gallery," brandonbandy.com.

2 I want to thank Stewart Copeland, director of the ARTs lab at the University of New Mexico, Jessica Metz, Daniel Neves, and the Department of Art at UNM for making this project possible.

3 I'm deeply indebted to Mark Pilkington both personally and professionally for his guidance and inspiration. His book *Mirage Men* is the definitive account of the use of UFOs by military and intelligence agencies to conduct psychological operations. See Mark Pilkington, *Mirage Men: An Adventure into Paranoia, Espionage, Psychological Warfare, and UFOs* (London: Orion Books, 2010).

4 The Bennewitz story is most comprehensively documented in Greg Bishop, *Project Beta: The Story of the First US Space Contact* (New York: Paraview Press, 2005).

5 *Army Field Manual*, FM 3-13.4, "Army Support to Military Deception," Department of the Army, February 2019; *Army Field Manual*, FM 90-2, "Battlefield Deception," Department of the Army, October 3, 1988.

6 "Summary of Remarks by Mr. Allen W. Dulles at the National Alumni Conference of the Graduate Council of Princeton University, Hot Springs, Va., April 10, 1953," General CIA Records, Cia-Rdp70-00058r000200050069-9.

7 Timothy Melley, "Brainwashed! Conspiracy Theory and Ideology in the Postwar United States," *New German Critique* 103 (2008).

8 For the history of MKUltra, see John Marks, *The Search for the "Manchurian Candidate": The CIA and Mind Control* (New York: Times Books, 1979); Stephen Kinzer, *Poisoner in Chief: Sidney Gottlieb and the CIA Search for Mind Control* (New York: St. Martin's Griffin, 2020); and H. P. Albarelli Jr., *A Terrible Mistake: The Murder of Frank Olson and the CIA's Secret Cold War Experiments* (Walterville, OR: Trine Day, 2009).

9 For Bledsoe's work on facial recognition, see Stephanie Dick, "The Standard Head," in Gerardo Con Diaz and Jeffrey Yost,

eds., *Just Code* (Baltimore: Johns Hopkins University Press, 2025); Kashmir Hill, *Your Face Belongs to Us: A Secretive Start-up's Quest to End Privacy as We Know It* (New York: Random House, 2023); and Shaun Raviv, "The Secret History of Facial Recognition," *Wired*, January 21, 2020.

10 For MKUltra Subproject 94, see Central Intelligence Agency, *MKULTRA DOC_0000017497*, archive.org.

11 CIA memo, November 22, 1961.

12 José Manuel Rodríguez Delgado, *Physical Control of the Mind: Toward a Psychocivilized Society* (New York: Harper & Row, 1969).

13 Memorandum for the Record, Subject: Project MKULTRA, Sub-project no. 94, November 22, 1961, CIA Document 00693625.

14 CIA memo for chief of the Technical Services Division, February 7, 1964, https://www.cia.gov/readingroom/docs/CIA-RDP78-04727A000300130088-0.pdf.

15 Daniel Crevier, *AI: The Tumultuous History of the Search for Artificial Intelligence* (New York: Basic Books, 1993), 133; Simone Natale, *Deceitful Media: Artificial Intelligence and Social Life After the Turing Test* (Oxford: Oxford University Press, 2021).

16 Joseph Weizenbaum, *Computer Power and Human Reason: From Judgment to Calculation* (New York: W. H. Freeman, 1976).

17 Joseph Weizenbaum, "ELIZA: A Computer Program for the Study of Natural Language Communication Between Man and Machine," *Communications of the ACM* 9, no. 1 (January 1966).

18 Crevier, *AI*, 139.

19 An illuminating series of blog posts on this topic can be found here: "Again Theory: A Forum on Language, Meaning, and Intent in the Time of Stochastic Parrots," *In the Moment* (blog), September 6, 2023, critinq.wordpress.com.

20 See, for example, superic, "Atheist Nightmare," YouTube, April 26, 2006.

21 For the neuroscience of magic, see Stephen L. Macknik et al., *Sleights of Mind: What the Neuroscience of Magic Reveals About Our Everyday Deceptions* (New York: Picador, 2011).

22 Ramsey Dukes, *S.s.o.t.b.m.e. Revised: An Essay on Magic* (London: Mouse That Spins, 2001), 9.

23 I'm using "magick" here as a shorthand for occult traditions that see the relationship between perception and reality as far

more complicated than a materialist paradigm can account for. Although the word "magick" is most often associated with Aleister Crowley, I am invoking it more in reference to the philosophies of the proto-surrealist artist Austin Spare and the tradition of "chaos magick" that his work would later inspire.

24 I'd like to thank Aaron Gach of the Center for Tactical Magic for being my guide to all things magical and magickal.

25 John Mulholland, *John Mulholland's Book of Magic* (Mineola, NY: Dover, 2001).

26 John Mulholland, "Magicians Scoff," *Popular Science*, September 1952, 96.

27 For a biography of Mulholland, see Ben Robinson and John Nicholls Booth, *The Magician: John Mulholland's Secret Life* (Somerville, MA: Lybrary.com, 2008). For Mulholland's work on MKUltra, see Albarelli, *A Terrible Mistake*.

28 There was a magic trick of sorts embedded in the name of this company. It's easiest to see by copy/pasting the name into a text box with a serif font.

29 The way I've told the story here is slightly fictionalized. The exact timing of the ghost-plane operation in the context of the Cuban missile crisis isn't known. The account here is based on the recollections of Gene Poteat, "Stealth, Countermeasures, and ELINT, 1960–1975," *Studies in Intelligence* 42, no. 1 (1998).

30 See Tyler Rogoway, "Adversary Drones Are Spying on the US and the Pentagon Acts Like They're UFOs," *War Zone*, April 16, 2021, twz.com; "Are Some of the UFOs Navy Pilots Are Encountering Actually Airborne Radar Reflectors?," *War Zone*, December 1, 2019, twz.com.

31 For the intersection of psychology and magic, see Peter Lamont and Richard Wiseman, *Magic in Theory: An Introduction to the Theoretical and Psychological Elements of Conjuring* (Hatfield: University of Hertfordshire Press, 1999).

32 Bruce Wexler, *Brain and Culture: Neurobiology, Ideology, Social Change* (Cambridge, MA: MIT Press, 2006), 39.

33 Bernard Claverie and François du Cluzel, "The Cognitive Warfare Concept," 2022, available at innovationhub-act.org.

34 Bobby Allyn, Sylvia Goodman, and Dara Kerr, "Inside the TikTok Documents: Stripping Teens and Boosting 'Attractive' People,'" NPR, October 16, 2024.

35 David Z. Morris, "Ashley Madison Used Chatbots to Lure Cheaters, Then Threatened to Expose Them When They Complained," *Fortune*, July 10, 2016.

36 Sébastien Bubeck et al., "Sparks of Artificial General Intelligence: Early Experiments with GPT-4," arXiv, March 22, 2023.

37 Kevin Roose, "Can AI Be Blamed for a Teen's Suicide?," *New York Times*, October 23, 2024.

6. The Archives of the Future

1 The ideas in this essay are deeply indebted to a long series of conversations with Gideon Jacobs, who has been spending a lot of time thinking about the theological implications of a post-AI visual culture. See, for example, Gideon Jacobs, "Player One and Main Character," *Los Angeles Review of Books*, April 17, 2025, and "Thou Shalt Not Make Images—but What if AI Does?," *Document*, April 17, 2025, documentjournal.com.

2 Ezekiel 1:16 KJV; 2 Kings 2:11 KJV.

3 Jeffrey J. Kripal, "Shooting Down Souls … Good Luck with That," *Debrief*, February 16, 2024, thedebrief.org.

4 I should say at the outset that I don't have any particular commitment to any of these threads. I have no particular commitment to the so-called nuts and bolts interpretation of the phenomena (which posits UFOs as advanced machines from other worlds), nor to the psychological/symbolic interpretation (positing that they are psychical or meta-psychical objects). Nonetheless, it is a fact that people see UFOs (broadly defined), that those sightings often have profound consequences for those who encounter them, and, most importantly for the purposes of this essay, that there are sometimes photographs.

5 As for whether UFOs are "real," I remain agnostic. Do people see strange things in the sky? Absolutely. Is the line between what we see and what we imagine we're seeing completely blurry? Absolutely. Furthermore, as my friend Pete Skafish points out, if you asked 99 percent of people in 99 percent of places in 99 percent of human history if there was weird stuff flying around the skies, they'd look at you like you're a complete idiot because yeah, obviously. Duh. I'll conclude this note by quoting Erik Davis to say

that "the question of whether or not UFOs are 'real' is, alternately, too crude and too philosophically taxing to broach." Erik Davis, *Techgnosis* (New York: Harmony Books, 1998).

6 The photographs of "Asket" and "Nera" turned out to be photographs of guests on the Dean Martin television show.

7 Exodus 20:4, KJV, cf. Deuteronomy 5:8.

8 Michael Shaw, "The Concept of the Image in the Old and New Testaments," in Krešimir Purgar, ed., *The Palgrave Handbook of Image Studies* (London: Palgrave Macmillan, 2021), 26; I don't want to go down a rabbit hole discussing all the theological subtleties associated with the Second Commandment. (While Yahweh seemed to prohibit his followers from making idolatrous images, he also instructed Moses to adorn the Ark of the Covenant with two cherubim, among many other examples.) But a few things seem clear. At minimum, the relationship between images and the divine is complicated.

9 Exodus 33:20.

10 This account is, of course, astoundingly simplified. My aim isn't to conduct an exegesis so much as to set up a few different ways of thinking about the relationship between images and truth over history.

11 I differentiate UFO sightings with photography as a native genre from "abduction" or "close encounter" stories, where drawing is a much more important medium.

12 This passage is an almost criminally negligent oversimplification of the actual history. For a most robust account, see Lorraine Daston and Peter Galison, "The Image of Objectivity," in "Seeing Science," special issue, *Representations* 40 (Autumn 1992): 81–128.

13 Allan Sekula, "Dismantling Modernism, Reinventing Documentary (Notes on the Politics of Representation)," *Massachusetts Review* 19, no. 4 (Winter 1978): 859–83.

14 Judith Butler, "Endangered/Endangering: Schematic Racism and White Paranoia," in Robert Cooding-Williams, ed., *Reading Rodney King / Reading Urban Uprising* (New York: Routledge, 1993).

15 W. J. T. Mitchell, "Cloning Terror: The War of Images 2001–04," in Diarmuid Costello and Dominic Willsdon, eds., *The Life and Death of Images: Ethics and Aesthetics* (Ithaca, NY: Cornell University Press, 2008).

16 What's more, any photo taken with a smartphone is now preprocessed with so many machine-learning algorithms designed to "enhance" it that nearly every photograph taken by a human has become a hybrid photograph–AI construction.
17 Some might quibble that the link between the AI-generated photograph and its training data forms an index, but I don't want to go that far into the weeds on this topic.
18 There's a subtle possible point here about hallucinations not simply being things AI gets "wrong" or "makes up"—it's more accurate to say that AI "makes up" everything; it just happens to sometimes accidentally stumble upon statements that appear to be tethered to reality.
19 See Ben Davis, "A New Genre of Bad A.I. Art Takes Shape: Nature Slop," *Artnet News*, November 24, 2024, news.artnet.com.
20 "Trump Will Not Concede MS-13 Letters Were Digitally Added," *New York Times*, April 30, 2025.
21 Amy Kremer, x.com, October 3, 2024.
22 Jason Koebler, "Where Facebook's AI Slop Comes From," *404 Media*, August 6, 2024, 404media.co.

Conclusion

1 "Madison Square Garden Uses Facial Recognition to Ban Its Owner's Enemies," *New York Times*, December 22, 2022.
2 Rindala Alajaji, "She Got an Abortion. So a Texas Cop Used 83,00 Cameras to Track Her Down," Electronic Frontier Foundation, May 30, 2025, eff.org.
3 Spencer Ackerman, "US to Continue 'Signature Strikes' on people Suspected of Terrorist Links," *Guardian*, July 2, 2016.
4 See Daniel Boorstin, *The Image: A Guide to Pseudo-Events in America* (New York: Vintage, 1992); Jacques Ellul, *Propaganda: The Formation of Men's Attitudes* (New York: Knopf, 1965).

Index

Index